The Busy IT Manager's Guide to Data Recovery

No IT manager or worker enjoys being woken up in the middle of the night over a system fault. But arguably the worst way to be awakened is over a situation where data loss has occurred – and the recovery is going wrong.

The Busy IT Manager's Guide to Data Recovery takes a razor focus on the details IT managers (and their teams) responsible for data recovery and resiliency within their business need to be aware of in the design of robust data protection systems. This book covers key architectural requirements of a data resilient system and the types of technology a business can deploy for data protection that maximises the potential for a successful recovery.

With cyber-attacks being a daily challenge for IT and business now, the book also takes an in-depth look at the special considerations companies need to take in order to guarantee the recoverability of data after a destructive cyber event.

Regardless of whether your IT infrastructure runs on-premises or in the public cloud, this book gives you the information you need to plan and run a successful data recovery solution that meets your business needs.

Preston de Guise has been working with data recovery products for his entire career – designing, implementing, and supporting solutions for governments, universities, and businesses ranging from SMEs to Fortune 500 companies. This broad exposure to industry verticals and business sizes has enabled Preston to understand not only the technical requirements of data protection and recovery, but the management and procedural aspects too.

IT Pro Practice Notes

Practical Guide to IT Problem Management
By Andrew Dixon
2022

Cybertax: Managing the Risks and Results
By George K. Tsantes, James Ransome
2023

Agile Software Development
By Peter Wlodarczak
2024

The Busy IT Manager's Guide to Data Recovery
By Preston de Guise
2024

The Busy IT Manager's Guide to Data Recovery

Preston de Guise

CRC Press
Taylor & Francis Group
Boca Raton London New York

CRC Press is an imprint of the
Taylor & Francis Group, an **informa** business
AN AUERBACH BOOK

First edition published 2024
by CRC Press
2385 NW Executive Center Drive, Suite 320, Boca Raton FL 33431

and by CRC Press
4 Park Square, Milton Park, Abingdon, Oxon, OX14 4RN

CRC Press is an imprint of Taylor & Francis Group, LLC

© 2024 Taylor & Francis Group, LLC

ISBN: 978-1-032-62494-5 (hbk)
ISBN: 978-1-032-45125-1 (pbk)
ISBN: 978-1-032-62495-2 (ebk)

DOI: 10.1201/9781032624952

Typeset in Sabon
by SPi Technologies India Pvt Ltd (Straive)

For Daz.

Contents

Acknowledgements

Even with a single author, any technical book is still in its own way a group effort. Technical books are a distillation of experiences covering sometimes decades in the industry, and the lessons learned from those experiences have been distilled into this book. Those experiences aren't attained in isolation; each one came with businesses and individuals attached.

Learning about rigorous adherence to change control? That was a shared lesson between a customer's infrastructure administrator and me during the Sydney Olympics in 2000, when we were 11 hours through a 12-hour change window, only to find out the paperwork hadn't been fully signed, and being required by the datacentre owner to roll back the entire change. Learning about checking recovery steps before running them? That was me, accidentally recovering /dev from a Linux system onto a Solaris backup server, simultaneously failing to recover a colleague's laptop in time for a business trip, *and* earning myself a weekend sleeping in the office while I rebuilt and recovered the server – then the laptop.

Data recoverability may seem like an IT function, but at the end of the day it's a very human function, too. We recover data not because it's fun, but because it's needed, and at some point it is always a human that needs the recovery. It's been my privilege to work with so many people over the years who are passionate about making sure those recoveries *work* when they're needed. There are too many to call out by name, and confidentiality would require me to not name some at all, so I'll suffice it to say: if you've worked with me on data recovery activities at any point in the past, I have treasured the insights you've offered me.

I also owe special thanks to Udi Shemer for kindly providing a thorough and insightful review to the draft of this book – his comments and feedback, as always, are greatly appreciated.

And finally, thank *you* for being interested in reading this book about data recovery. May it help you on your journey.

Chapter 1

Introduction

1.1 WHAT'S THIS BOOK ABOUT?

Have you ever watched a TV show that freeze-frames precisely at a point when disaster happens, and has the main character opine, "You may be wondering how I got here", before rewinding time for 24 or 48 hours and then launching into the story?

If you have, you've experienced that moment we all feel when getting a call in the middle of the night to say that a data recovery situation has gone wrong. While some data recovery situations may fail in truly random, unexpected ways, many failure situations have been engineered into the data protection posture of the business.

Regardless of whether you're an IT manager *accountable* for data recovery, or an IT worker *responsible* for data recovery, the goal of this book is to help you attain a more reliable data recovery posture within your business. While some of that may be driven by technology, it also comes down to understanding common challenges when planning and implementing resilient data protection systems.

 LESSON ONE: It's *when*, not *if* bad things will happen and a recovery is required.

1.2 SIX ESSENTIAL GAPS

Chances are, there will be gaps in your data recovery preparedness. While the goal of this book is to help you fix that, you can rest assured that you're in good company. Most businesses have gaps in

DOI: 10.1201/9781032624952-1

their data recovery preparedness – so while your competitors may be doing some things right in comparison to you, you'll likely find that you're also doing some things right in comparison to them.

After more than 25 years of specialising in data protection, I've noticed there are six essential gaps that keep on appearing in data protection models – regardless of the business, its industry vertical, size, platform model, or who runs the IT environment. Let's review what those gaps are:

1. Roles and responsibilities are poorly defined for data protection activities.
2. Systems are not architected for data resilience.
3. The ability to protect and recover data is not a first-class citizen in the metrics for choosing new systems, workloads, and workload placement.
4. IT functions and systems are not properly associated with business functions.
5. Processes and documentation are not seen as first-class activities within data protection (or IT).
6. Data protection budgets are allocated from the IT budget rather than out of the business budget.

The number of gaps and their scope will vary from business to business; it will be rare to encounter a business that has fully eliminated all of these.

 LESSON TWO: The journey to a resilient data recovery model within your organisation starts by recognising the gaps you have in your model.

1.3 MAKING USE OF THIS BOOK

To recover data, you must first have protected it. So while the focus of this book is on data recovery, we must first spend time considering some best practices to *protecting* data in the first place.

That's why Chapter 2 is titled "Understanding Data Resilience"; it will take you through the key things you need to understand, architect, and otherwise plan for to have a reliable data recovery solution within your environment. These are *technology agnostic* (or at least *product* agnostic) topics that'll give you the fundamentals you need as an IT manager, architect, or leader for integrating data resilience into your holistic service model. This chapter can serve as a guided tour, regardless of whether you're just starting to plan data recovery solutions in your business, or want to review an architecture and solution already in place.

Chapter 3, "Enabling Recoverability", will look at technical and financial approaches to data protection. Yes, financial considerations are important! After all, the bulk of your business's data footprint can easily end up residing in data protection copies, which makes it important to get it right. We'll examine various technical, procedural, and financial considerations, and how each of them helps you provide data recovery solutions to the business.

Chapter 4, "Building Recovery into Cyber Resilience", looks at the important role a strong data recovery model can provide in helping your business survive a destructive cyber-attack. While the topic of Cyber Resilience is almost universally treated as one of *Security and Risk*, if you don't architect for data recoverability in response to a cyber-attack, you're mistakenly assuming that all attacks will be blocked.

1.4 RECOVERY CATEGORIES

A data protection system can be used to facilitate a variety of recovery types. In general, we can categorise these recovery types as follows:

1. Operational
2. Long-term (compliance)
3. Disaster
4. Business continuity
5. Data re-use
6. Audit (test)

Each recovery category has its own service level objectives (SLOs), criteria, and stakeholders. SLOs will be primarily focused on recovery point objectives (RPOs) and recovery time objectives (RTOs). However, these objectives, criteria, and stakeholders are not universally the same within a category; within a category, those elements will shift depending on the criticality of each dataset to the business, and any externally imposed requirements.

Not every dataset within the business will need recovery capabilities provisioned from each of the above categories. For instance, dev/test systems may get short-term operational backups, but are unlikely to require long-term (compliance) recoveries. Virtual Desktop Infrastructure (VDI) platforms spun up from templates may require no recovery capabilities beyond disaster recoverability for the templated virtual machines.

Table 1.1 outlines *some* of the objectives and criteria that apply to each of the recovery categories above.

It's common to confuse disaster recoveries and business continuity. The difference between the two is usually simple: disaster recoveries are invoked by IT, and wherever possible should be automated. Business continuity though is invoked by the business, and is process-driven. They won't just be for individual workloads or systems, but entire business functions (or the entire business) and will have significantly more moving parts requiring coordination than just IT systems. For this reason, while it is typical to expect

Table 1.1 Criteria of recovery categories

Category	RPO	RTO	Granularity	Cost focus
Operational	Seconds to days	Seconds to days	Fine/detailed	Recovery speed
Long-term (compliance)	Typically months or years, sometimes weeks, rarely days	Days to weeks	Variable – can be fine/detailed (individual files) or low (complete workloads)	Storage volume
Disaster	Zero to hours	Zero to hours	Workload	Recovery speed
Business Continuity	Hours to days	Hours to days	Business function	Recovery speed
Data re-use	Typically days	Typically hours to days	Typically system or workload	Ease of retrieval
Audit (test)	Any (matches test purpose)	Any (matches test purpose)	Any (matches test purpose)	N/A

disaster recovery operations to complete in sometimes seconds or less (e.g., automated failover of volume storage groups in a metro cluster), business continuity recoveries are usually measured in hours or days, depending on the scope of the invocation and the preparedness of the business.

1.5 SIMPLE, CHEAP, FLEXIBLE

When considering how you can achieve data recoverability within your business, it's worth keeping in mind these three words: simple, cheap, and flexible.
But note you can only ever choose two.

 LESSON THREE: Simple, cheap, flexible. When it comes to data recoverability, you can only ever choose two.

Simple can be cheap, but it's not going to be cheap *and* flexible. You can have flexible and simple, but it's not going to be cheap. And by extension, you can always have cheap, but you'll always have to choose between simple and flexible. Anyone who tells you that you can have all three probably also has a bridge they'd like to sell you.

What's the right choice? It's the one that meets the most business objectives for data recoverability for your organisation. There's a logical consequence of this statement: the right choice for a small business can be entirely different to the right choice for a mid-sized business, which can again be entirely different to the right choice for an enterprise. The right choice can even be different between two comparably sized businesses in the same industry.

It's always good to see and understand how other businesses handle data recoverability, but keep in mind your plans and architecture must focus on what is right for *your* business. As you move on to the next chapter, apply that lens of 'for my business' to the topics discussed.

Chapter 2

Understanding data resilience

2.1 RACI APPROACHES TO DATA RECOVERABILITY

In February 2017, GitLab posted a blog article that outlined their root cause analysis into an issue they encountered at the end of the previous month. In it, they provided details for an incident which resulted in data loss across an estimated 5,000 hosted projects that had committed new content between 17:20 and 00:00 UTC on 31 January. While their commitment to transparency in their post-mortem was admirable, the issues they outlined demonstrated a lack of maturity (at least at that time) in their data resilience process. They noted in a section titled "Problem 2: restoring GitLab. com took over 18 hours" the following sequence:

1) **Why did restoring GitLab.com take so long?** – GitLab. com had to be restored using a copy of the staging database. This was hosted on slower Azure VMs in a different region.

2) **Why was the staging database needed for restoring GitLab.com?** – Azure disk snapshots were not enabled for the database servers, and the periodic database backups using pg_dump were not working.

3) **Why could we not fail over to the secondary database host?** – The secondary database's data was wiped as part of restoring database replication. As such it could not be used for disaster recovery.

4) **Why could we not use the standard backup procedure?** – The standard backup procedure uses pg_dump to perform a

DOI: 10.1201/9781032624952-2

logical backup of the database. This procedure failed silently because it was using PostgreSQL 9.2, while GitLab.com runs on PostgreSQL 9.6.

5) **Why did the backup procedure fail silently?** – Notifications were sent upon failure, but because of the Emails being rejected there was no indication of failure. The sender was an automated process with no other means to report any errors.

6) **Why were the Emails rejected?** – Emails were rejected by the receiving mail server due to the Emails not being signed using DMARC.

7) **Why were Azure disk snapshots not enabled?** – We assumed our other backup procedures were sufficient. Furthermore, restoring these snapshots can take days.

8) **Why was the backup procedure not tested on a regular basis?** – Because there was no ownership, as a result nobody was responsible for testing this procedure.

"Postmortem of database outage of January 31", GitLab.com. February 10, 2017. https://about.gitlab.com/blog/2017/02/10/postmortem-of-database-outage-of-january-31/

The technical aspects of the GitLab outage are interesting, but the most relevant part of their root cause analysis is this: "Because there was no ownership, as a result nobody was responsible for testing this procedure."

Data resilience starts *before* you get to technology. It starts with people and processes, and to get these two right, you should start by developing an agreed matrix for data protection outlining:

- Who is Responsible?
- Who is Accountable?
- Who is Consulted?
- Who is Informed?

In systems architecture, this is referred to as a RACI chart. When developing a RACI chart for data resilience, you'll need to consider potentially many different scenarios covering initial data protection and the way in which the business needs data recovered. These will depend on a variety of non-technical factors, including workload type, workload criticality, and workload location. To be specific, it will be RACI *charts*, plural, not singular, that will be required.

For example, following are three potential RACI charts for different data protection scenarios within the same business (Tables 2.1 to 2.3).

Table 2.1 RACI chart for unclassified ("default") workloads

	Backup	*Recovery*	*Disaster recovery*
Responsible	Backup Administrator	Application and Platform Administrators	Application and Platform Administrators
Accountable	IT Manager	IT Manager	CIO
Consulted	Application and Platform Administrators, Business	Business	Business
Informed	End Users	End Users	End Users

Table 2.2 RACI chart for Oracle workloads

	Backup	*Recovery*	*Disaster recovery*
Responsible	Backup Administrator	Oracle Administrator	Oracle Administrator
Accountable	IT Manager	IT Manager	CIO
Consulted	Oracle Administrator	Business	Business
Informed	End Users	End Users	End Users

Table 2.3 RACI chart for Microsoft SQL Server workloads

	Backup	*Recovery*	*Disaster recovery*
Responsible	Backup Administrator	Backup Administrator	SQL Administrator
Accountable	IT Manager	IT Manager	CIO
Consulted	SQL Administrator	Business	Business
Informed	End Users	End Users	End Users

In these examples, you'll note that depending on the type of workload, the responsibility for recovery or disaster recovery changes, but the responsibility for the backup operation remains the same. This would be typical of situations where a centralised service runs all backup operations. While IT administration staff are *responsible* for the various operations performed though, it will typically be management team members who are *accountable* for the functioning of the environment. Returning to the GitLab example, you might say that the core problem was a lack of an *accountable* person to ensure operational ownership wasn't forgotten about. It almost goes without saying but should be noted regardless: a RACI chart should cite *roles*, not *names*.

 LESSON FOUR: A machine can neither be responsible nor accountable for data protection.

The examples above are based on different workload types – generic, Oracle, and SQL Server. That's one way to do RACI charts, but you might say they're *all* generic for data protection operations as they don't look beyond the workload type. At some point, as we move up the stack into *business functions*, RACI charts that deal with data protection and recovery operations should directly categorise roles for functions, not workloads – e.g., you would have a RACI chart for "Customer sales", not "Oracle", "SQL", and so on. After all, the business doesn't really care about what the backing technology of a business function is – what they care about is the business function itself, and so you need to plan recovery around business functions. We will go into this in more detail later.

2.2 ARCHITECTING FOR DATA RESILIENCE

Comprehensive data resilience is not intrinsic to workloads unless you architect and build it into the offering. This is regardless of whether you're operating a workload on-premises or in a public cloud.

Resilient Workload			
Fault Tolerance	Availability	Redundancy	Recoverability

Figure 2.1 The FARR model for resilient workloads.

It is usual for some platforms to offer a certain level of resilience. Most on-premises block- and file-based storage arrays support a variety of redundant array of independent disks (RAID) levels, and on-premises object storage usually offers a selection of erasure coding. Likewise, public cloud object storage usually has a particular *resilience* stated, but we'll explain shortly why this isn't the full picture.

To achieve a data-resilient architecture, it is necessary to design based on four key concepts:

- Fault tolerance
- Availability
- Redundancy
- Recoverability

These four pillars (which will be referred to as the FARR model) combined allow you to reach a state where your workloads are resilient (Figure 2.1).

Each of these features offer a unique attribute and functionality towards resiliency. When all four are used *effectively*, you will be able to assert that you have achieved workload resiliency.

You might say that regardless of whether we're talking fault tolerance, availability, redundancy, or recoverability, there is always a single guiding principle to follow when architecting for data resilience. That principle is that a resilient data architecture requires the elimination of any element as a single point of failure.

 LESSON FIVE: Resiliency can come only from the synergistic application of all four pillars. It cannot come from a subset of pillars, no matter how strongly you build them up.

So, let's look at those four key pillars.

2.2.1 Fault tolerance

Fault tolerance refers to the fundamental protection against individual component failure within a platform. This covers areas such as:

- Storage arrays that use RAID or erasure coding
- Memory systems with Error Correcting Code (ECC)
- System cooling systems that can survive the loss of a fan
- Platforms that can survive the loss of one or more CPUs

Fault tolerance is geared towards reducing the amount of *immediate* repair operations to be performed within systems due to atomic component failure. A storage platform may be able to lose multiple hard drives or flash storage units without loss of data based on the RAID levels or erasure coding, and replacement parts may not be immediately required; hot spares can allow for fault tolerance levels to be repaired automatically.

As the priority of a workload increases to the business, the fault tolerance of the system(s) used to run that workload for the business should also increase.

2.2.2 Availability

You might think of the availability aspect of the FARR model as being "Schrödinger's Data". Availability refers to both the data and the systems that are used to interact with the data. If you cannot observe or interact with your data, can you say it still exists? From the perspective of the users of the workload the data depends on, the answer may be a firm 'no'.

A lack of availability doesn't (usually) result in a data loss situation, but it does result in data being *inaccessible*, and for users of the data, there will be little differentiation. Depending on the criticality of a workload, in situations where data remains unavailable for an extended period, it may be necessary to treat it like a data loss situation and find a way to restore alternate copies of the data.

Availability is often considered from the perspective of network or data path perspectives, and this can apply not only to connections within a datacentre, but also to connections in a cloud. Within the datacentre, typical availability considerations include:

- Multi-pathing for storage
- Multiple network connections:

- Two or more connections from a server to the switching and
- Redundant switching
- Multiple connections between datacentres

Within the public cloud, the availability discussion can cover link availability (e.g., multiple connections between your datacentres and the internet), and it can also cover in-cloud service availability. For instance, you may deploy a service into Amazon Web Services (AWS)'s Asia/Sydney zone, but what happens if your link to this region is temporarily lost even though the rest of AWS is still working?

Availability can also encompass *performance* and *responsiveness*. An Australian investment organisation once polled its users and its IT department to gather information on how reliable the IT systems were for the business. The IT department gave computer systems and storage platforms a strong thumbs-up for reliability because they looked at system 'uptime' and deemed it to show successful availability. On the other hand, the end users ranked those same systems as being quite unreliable since services were often so slow that they were deemed unusable.

Availability, therefore, is more than a technical measurement – in fact, it refers to whether the data or systems are *usable* by the business.

2.2.3 Redundancy

While redundancy can sometimes be synonymous with fault tolerance, and can also play into availability, here we consider redundancy to be holistic system redundancy. That is, while we would look at surviving component failures within a single system as *fault tolerance*, we can look at redundancy as being able to survive the loss of a much higher-order system. We use 'system' here because redundancy could cover a variety of different platforms: you might have redundancy in storage, redundancy in compute services, redundancy in networking, and so on.

A typical form of redundancy when we consider higher-order systems is *clustering*. The traditional form of clustering comes from when services mostly ran directly on bare metal hosts. In earlier IT contexts, this might have been clustered database servers and clustered fileservers; while these types of workloads can still be found, the most common modern context for clustering within on-premises environments is hypervisor clusters – e.g., VMware vCenter and vSphere clusters. These two scenarios are not mutually exclusive however: virtualised mission-critical workloads might also have application-level clustering applied to them.

You might say that while fault tolerance is designed to provide protection against atomic component failure, redundancy is designed to provide protection against catastrophic system failure. RAID is unlikely to provide adequate protection against, say, someone knocking over a server rack in a datacentre. Well-architected redundant systems, however, would. This is sometimes referred to as *limiting the blast radius* – i.e., ensuring that failures are logically and physically contained. In the previous example, redundant systems design would demand that systems which can failover for one another would not be in the same rack.

2.2.4 Recoverability

Fault tolerance, availability, and redundancy all exist to attempt to curtail data loss – to limit the situations in which data loss can occur. Yet they cannot provide total proof against data loss.

LESSON SIX: **Nothing corrupts faster than a mirror.**

At some point, something bad *will* happen resulting in a data loss situation. A user will delete a file they didn't mean to. An application will crash while saving a file and erase its content. A virus will encrypt data on a fileserver. A DBA will accidentally recover a backup from three weeks ago over the production rather than the test database. A fire will break out in a cloud provider's datacentre.

An architecture that focuses on achieving data resilience will also include provision for recovery of data should it be necessary. In most businesses, the recovery aspect of a FARR architecture will be used for secondary scenarios – e.g., for repopulating development copies of databases, testing, or compliance. But ultimately, recoveries exist as a last line of insurance in a resilient data architecture.

2.2.5 The bedrock

In discussing pillars of data resilience, it's worth bringing your attention to the foundations. As numerous parables relate, even the best house in the world is unlikely to survive if it's built on sand. So, the FARR model relies on a foundational bedrock to give it stability, and that bedrock is *robustness*.

"Robustness has traditionally been thought of as the ability of a software-reliant system to keep working, consistent with its specifications, despite the presence of internal failures, faulty inputs, or external stresses, over a long period of time."

"Tactics and Patterns for Software Robustness", Rick Kazman, July 25 2022, Carnegie Mellon University Software Engineering Institute SEI Blog, https://insights.sei.cmu.edu/blog/tactics-and-patterns-for-software-robustness/

Beyond the theory, the *impact* of robustness is perhaps best explained from the end-user perspective. What happens when their Office application crashes? Let's say a user is working on an important spreadsheet – what happens if they click 'save' and the application hangs, requiring a forced crash? When they re-open the spreadsheet application, one of a few different scenarios might happen:

- The file is empty
- The file is corrupted
- The file is subtly corrupted (they may not even notice it for days or weeks after)
- The file is accurate to the last save *before* the crash
- The file is accurate to the time *of* the crash

This is the core of data robustness. For instance, in the example of saving a spreadsheet, how does the application handle that save? On even a simple inspection there are at least four approaches:

- Approach one – it appends deltas to the file
- Approach two – it uses a format that allows it to both append new blocks and perform targeted updates of existing blocks

- Approach three – it:
  - Writes a new file
  - Verifies the file has been written successfully, then
  - Deletes the old file, and
  - Renames the new file to the old.
- Approach four – it:
  - Writes a new file
  - Verifies the file has been written successfully, then
  - Creates a copy of the newly written file and verifies it (to provide recoverability should the subsequent rename operation fail)
  - Deletes the old file
  - Renames one of the copies to the old file name, and
  - Deletes the spare copy.

Of the four approaches, the methods described in three and four provide a much higher level of robustness. If the application crashes while it's saving the file, the previous version of the file was not open and therefore should still be OK.

Approach four is engineered to a higher level of robustness than approach three. Approach three is robust in the saving of data but *assumes* operating system robustness when it comes to file operations. The fourth approach, on the other hand, offers robustness in saving and builds in contingency for an operating system/filesystem error when the file it has written is renamed.

 LESSON SEVEN: Fault tolerance, availability, redundancy, and recoverability all depend on robustness to deliver a reliable data protection architecture.

2.3 DATA, WORKLOADS, AND FUNCTIONS

This may come as a surprise to you, but when you work in data protection, your job is *not* the protection of data. The data is just part of the bigger picture.

This is a common mistake many businesses make when they're planning data recovery strategies: they assume that recovering the data is sufficient. For trivial data, such as file shares for home drives or general unstructured data, it *may* be as simple as this, but that can lull us into a false sense of security that data protection is only about data.

Businesses don't store data for the fun of it. There's a tangible cost associated with data storage, covering primary storage platforms, data protection storage, and the employee time associated with managing data. This means *data rarely exists in a vacuum.* Unless it's orphaned, data has a reason for existing within a business. Data has *purpose.*

So, what do we really protect in data protection?

To break this open, let's return to our previous example: *"trivial data, such as file shares or home shares"*. We've immediately got a higher-order classification here, even though it's a simple data example. The data is the files, and we can see there is a *workload* that could be referred to as file shares. The workload, therefore, encompasses the data, and an IT service – and therefore, the systems that provide that service. But is that all?

To answer this question, step outside of IT and ask yourself: "What is a file share to the business?" It's here we get to *business functions*, that is, for what purpose does a business use a workload and its data?

There is not always (in fact, rarely) a 1:1 relationship between a workload and a business function. A business function may be delivered by multiple workloads, as shown in Figure 2.2. A file share, then, does not of itself provide a business function, but it may contribute to a variety of business functions – any, in fact, that makes use of files.

In fact, a single workload is often likely to have more than one data set associated with it.

A corollary to this is that several business functions may overlap in their workload requirements; for instance, a vendor with "sales", "support", and "services" functions may see all three business

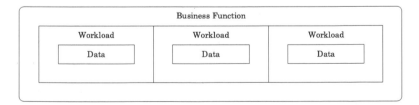

Figure 2.2 Relationship between data, workloads and business functions.

functions requiring workloads such as "file services", "email", and a "maintenance database".

Understanding the workload and the business function context is critical when planning data recovery, particularly as the complexity of the recovery increases. An individual file *may* be recovered without much consideration of the holistic workload or business function it is associated with, but by the time you're considering disaster recovery operations, the business function *must* be understood. (We will discuss this further in Section 2.6.1.)

As such, while you might say data protection is 'about' data, this is a blinkered view. Data protection is about the workloads, and the business functions. You'll protect data as part of that process, but you *must* approach recoverability from the perspectives of the workloads and business functions. Only by understanding and committing to this approach can we design for data resiliency and data recovery.

 LESSON EIGHT: You protect business functions and workloads. *Data* protection is a side-effect.

2.4 PROTECTION IS A CONTINUUM

Just as there are multiple architectural pillars for data resilience, there are multiple layers of data protection to be considered. These can be categorised by key characteristics such as the following:

- Cost:
  - What is the cost of procuring the protection? You'll likely want to amortise this for genuine comparisons – e.g., $/TB, or even $/TB/month. For capital purchases, you'll also want to understand the cost for maintenance/support renewals, too. (Subscription models typically include maintenance and support as part of the subscription fee.)
  - What is the cost of running the protection? This will include ancillary purchases, such as virtualisation platform resources, network links, egress fees, bandwidth requirements, and human costs – the number of employees required to install, configure, and run the solution.

- **Security**:
  - Can the protection meet your security requirements for data in-flight?
  - Can the protection meet your security requirements for data at-rest?
  - Can the protection meet your security requirements for access control?
- **Location**:
  - Is the protection *on-platform*, or *off-platform*? In other words, where does the protection copy exist, relative to the original data it is protecting?
- **Retention time**:
  - How long you can keep the protection copy for?
- **Service levels offered**:
  - Recovery Point Objective (RPO): To what granularity can you get your data back?
  - Recovery Time Objective (RTO): How long will it take you to get your data back?

It's important to provide data protection/recovery services to the various workloads and systems within the environment based on their criticality so that you can minimise costs and maximise efficiency. This is where you'll usually see teams refer to workload or protection categorisation levels such as "Gold", "Silver", and "Bronze" (or some other, similar categorisation).

When assigning protection categories, there are usually three broad types of systems (or platforms, depending on the on-premises vs in-cloud arrangement of the business) that require careful consideration. These are:

- **Business service systems**. These are the systems that directly enable business functions. For example, a shipment tracking database would be a business service system for a logistics/ freight company.
- **Business support systems**. These are the systems that enable the business to manage itself. For example, staff salary handling, operational procedures, and audit documentation.
- **IT operational service systems**. These are systems that provide the 'backbone' to business service and support systems. This includes DNS, directory services, and network switching.

Other systems (e.g., development and test systems) may not require careful consideration, and in some instances may not require data protection services at all. A general rule of thumb is this: if the recreation of a system cannot be wholly automated, and it requires more than 15 minutes employee time to deploy/configure, you should consider some data protection plan for it.

While the IT department will usually be solely responsible for categorising protection levels for the IT operational service systems, categorisation for the business service and business support systems must be a joint effort between the business and IT, if it is to be done correctly.

2.4.1 Replication

Replication as a concept refers to providing a physically separate copy of data. There are a few different ways that replication might work within a protection environment. These are outlined below.

2.4.1.1 Storage replication

When two or more storage arrays (storage area network (SAN) or network attached storage (NAS)) are used in an environment, storage replication can be used to ensure volumes are synchronised from one controller to another. If the source controller goes down (unscheduled or scheduled), systems accessing the replicated volumes can redirect (automatically or manually) to access the volume from the replica target controller.

Storage replication can be divided into two primary service levels – synchronous and asynchronous. These service levels set *how* a write is acknowledged by the storage platform. To understand the difference, let's consider some server writing to some storage target X that is replicating data to another storage target Y.

1. Synchronous replication:
   a. The server sends a write to storage target X.
   b. Storage target X writes the local copy.
   c. Storage target X passes the write to storage target Y.
   d. Storage target Y writes the data.
   e. Storage target Y advises X that the write has been completed.
   f. *Storage target X advises the server that the write is complete.*

2. Asynchronous replication:
   a. The server sends a write to storage target X.
   b. Storage target X writes the local copy.
   c. *Storage target X informs the server the write is complete.*
   d. Storage target X passes the write to storage target Y.
   e. Storage target Y writes the data.
   f. Storage target Y advises X that the write has been completed.

You will note in the above that the key differentiator is *when* the server is told that its write is complete. For synchronous replication, it's only when the data has been confirmed written to both storage targets. For asynchronous, it's when the data has been confirmed written to the *local* storage target. Synchronous replication works well within datacentres, other local area network (LAN) distances, and sometimes for metro area networks (MANs). However, asynchronous replication works best when there is lower bandwidth or higher latency between storage targets, such as across wide area networks (WANs). In this case, asynchronous replication will queue writes for transmission across the link between storage systems.

2.4.1.2 Application-controlled replication

A primary use case for this is database servers that perform 'log shipping' to keep a failover database in sync with an active database. Hypervisors that keep virtual machines synchronised between two sites (rather than relying on primary storage replication, above, to do so) may also perform application-level replication.

Application-controlled replication can sometimes feature a decision point between synchronous and asynchronous replication, similar to storage replication.

2.4.1.3 Protection copy replication

Protection copy replication refers to making copies of data protection copies. In other words, when a backup is performed against a filesystem or virtual machine, the backup is written to another storage platform entirely, regardless of whether that's block, filesystem, deduplication, tape, or object storage. However, without that *backup* being copied, the backup represents a single point of failure. If we think of backup as insurance, making copies of your backups is akin to ensuring your insurer has an underwriter.

Protection copy replication typically runs as part of a total backup workflow. That is, a protection policy will run, which will see assets within the business backed up to data protection storage. Once those backups have been completed, another step in the workflow will run to copy those backups to another location (and typically, another site). Protection copy replication will be typically referred to as either *replication* or *cloning*. (Less frequent terms include *duplication, twinning,* or *copying*.)

2.4.1.4 Ad-hoc replication

While the replication techniques discussed above may be more automated or at least initiated as part of a workflow, ad-hoc replication refers to situations where users or administrators manually trigger replication activities – e.g., running an 'rsync' (Linux/Unix) or 'robocopy' (Windows) command to synchronise or copy files between two folders.

2.4.1.5 How replication supports recoverability

The primary benefit offered by replication for ensuring data recoverability is by eliminating single points of failure for protected workloads. Replication can be crucial in enabling instantaneous or at least near-instantaneous disaster recovery, an essential requirement for mission-critical workloads in many organizations. Replication can allow for hosts to seamlessly switch between storage systems in the event of a path or storage system failure, without needing to conduct potentially time-consuming data recovery operations.

While replication delivers protection against loss of a copy of data, it does not in itself provide protection against data fallibility. Or, to put it more simply, replication follows the technical credence, "garbage in, garbage out" – the utility of replicated data is no different from the utility of the original data. Therefore, if the original data has been corrupted, or compromised with ransomware – or deleted – the same state will be passed on to the replica.

2.4.2 Snapshots

2.4.2.1 Snapshot overview

Whereas replication focuses on getting a physically separate copy of data, snapshots instead provide a *logically* separate copy of data, typically residing on the same storage controller as the original data.

The purpose of a snapshot is to capture a 'point in time' view of the affected workload (which may be block storage, file storage, virtual machines, or databases). There are several techniques for creating snapshots which we won't delve deeply into, but some considerations to be mindful of are:

1. Is the snapshot read-only, or read-write? Note that this refers to whether the *addressable snapshot* is read-only or read-write, not whether the original *workload* is writable.
   a. Read-only snapshots are useful for data protection purposes.
   b. Read-write snapshots offer more utility for data re-use scenarios. Their use for data protection is typically limited because they allow the snapshot data to be changed.
2. How is the original content updated? For example:
   a. Filesystem snapshots (e.g., NAS) tend to use techniques such as copy-on-write – i.e., you continue to write to the original location, but if you make a change to that location, you copy the data needed by the point-in-time snapshot to a journal or buffer area first, to preserve the content of the snapshot.
   b. Other snapshots (e.g., VMware's virtual machine snapshot functionality) tend to 'freeze' the virtual machine files and store new writes to journal files that can be either deleted (to roll the virtual machine back) or merged into the virtual machine (to release the snapshot) when an operation such as a backup has been completed.
3. Does the snapshot remain logically separate for its lifespan, or does it achieve eventual independence? In some cases, the snapshot might start off as a logical copy of the data, but be designed to eventually make a copy of *all* the original content, thus eventually providing a secondary copy (or clone) that allows the original to be deleted.

2.4.2.2 *How snapshots support recoverability*

Read-only snapshots enhance recoverability operations in most data protection environments. For instance, they are commonly used on NAS platforms to allow the generation of relatively high frequency point-in-time copies of a share. A business, for instance, might generate hourly snapshots of file shares for a 24-48 hour period, then phase these out to retaining half-daily snapshots for a week or more, before phasing *those* out to retain daily snapshots for a month or longer.

If integrated into file browsers (e.g., Windows Explorer), snapshots can allow for user self-serviced recovery, streamlining retrieval of documents without ever needing to initiate service requests or engaging backup and recovery teams.

Large corporate file shares also tend to be *dense*, with sometimes hundreds of millions or more files. Such filesystems are frequently problematic for backup and recovery services to traverse efficiently (limitations being primarily imposed by the walking of the filesystem, not the transfer speed of the data); in such situations, snapshots might be used to cover most operational recovery requirements (e.g., up to 30 days of retention), with backup and recovery services limited to *monthly* backups of shares for long-term/compliance retention.

Within virtual environments, snapshots serve another function by providing a 'frozen' copy of virtual machines for safe backup. Basic virtual machine snapshots deliver *crash consistency* – i.e., taking a virtual machine snapshot, backing it up and then restoring that backup will deliver a virtual machine that has seemingly just crashed and rebooted. However, hypervisors can work with some guest operating systems and application services to deliver *application-consistent* snapshots. For instance, taking a backup of an *application-consistent* snapshot of a Windows virtual machine running Microsoft SQL Server allows you to not only restore the virtual machine, but the database within it, since the database was readied for backup operations during the snapshot creation process.

Care should be taken to avoid using snapshots indefinitely – i.e., with retention times of months or years. Businesses that retain monthly snapshots for multiple years effectively sign themselves up for vendor lock-in, and make migration to alternate storage platforms problematic and expensive, no matter what benefits those platforms may offer.

One final caution is that whenever a snapshot resides on the same physical storage as the original data, the loss of that storage platform will destroy both the original and snapshot copies. For this reason, except for very short-term retention (e.g., when creating a read-only copy to generate a backup from) or low-importance data, both the original content *and* the snapshots should be replicated to a secondary storage platform so the storage platform isn't a single point of failure.

2.4.3 Continuous data protection

2.4.3.1 How continuous data protection works

Continuous data protection (CDP) aligns closely to replication, but it typically provides additional intelligence and functionality compared to the replication processes we've already discussed.

CDP usually works by inserting a *write splitter* in the IO stream between a system and its data storage. When writes are sent to the data storage layer, the writes are intercepted by the splitter, which writes one copy to the original intended destination, and another to a journal. This journal is then usually transmitted to one or more other locations to keep remote storage copies synchronised.

So far this sounds like replication. However, the difference in a CDP solution is that the journal history is kept in a *write-ordered* state, based on capacity or retention time limits. That means in addition to having an up-to-date replication copy, you can *rewind* the storage to an earlier IO state. You might think of CDP as being like a digital video recorder for your workload where at any point you can stop the current state and rewind a few minutes.

This can be sometimes integrated with application-consistency hooks – for instance, you might apply continuous replication of the storage for a Microsoft SQL database, but every 15 minutes coordinate a snapshot of the database. This means that you can 'rewind' the database to any point for crash-consistent recoveries, or any 15-minute marker for an application-consistent recovery.

2.4.3.2 How continuous data protection supports recoverability

CDP solutions allow for highly granular recovery scenarios. If using CDP for a virtual machine for instance, and you notice that the virtual machine became infected by a virus at 15:04, you could 'rewind' the virtual machine to 15:03 and see whether it's OK, or if it is still problematic, a few minutes earlier.

CDP does not come without cost, however. Whereas replication maintains a 1:1 copy of the replica source and destination, CDP maintains that copy *and* maintains a journal of previous writes which allow the 'rewind' functionality. If the workload you're protecting is not heavily written to, this may not require significant storage, but as the hourly or daily changes on the workload increases, so too do the storage requirements of the CDP journal.

The way in which journals are indexed and written allows for elasticity in the recovery granularity. Journal data might be kept allowing for recovery to any IO within a 24-hour period, then trimmed down to allow a granularity of an hour for the next few days, before being removed entirely. Thus, we might see protection as follows:

- CDP journaling to any IO for 24 hours
- Backup taken daily to provide basic operational recovery for 30 days
- CDP journaling reduced to a granularity of every 2 hours past the first day, kept for 7 days
- Backup taken monthly to provide compliance recovery for up to 7 years

CDP is usually integrated into data protection strategies for higher criticality workloads – it allows for much lower RPOs and RTOs than could be achieved with backup and recovery services, but at the cost of management and IO journals. Or, to put it another way, CDP can help you achieve the same zero or near-zero recovery point and time objectives as replication, but with point-in-time rollback capabilities as well.

2.4.4 Backup and recovery

2.4.4.1 How backup and recovery works

A backup is an *off*-platform copy of a workload within your environment that can be used to recover from even if the original workload is destroyed. Unlike many of the previously mentioned protection technologies, backups are fundamentally intended to be independent from the source systems and workloads being protected.

Backup and recovery services come in many topologies and levels of complexity. However, at their core, they consist of:

- A server that holds configuration, scheduling, and metadata
- Protection storage that backups are written to
- Clients or assets that are protected
- Agent software and proxies that coordinate transferring data from the clients/assets to the protection storage

Other elements can be present within a backup system – for example, many products (particularly those that evolved from tape) have architectural support for 'storage nodes'. These systems ease the load on the backup server by hosting protection storage and receiving backups for storage while still controlled by the primary backup server. When backup services support *direct* data paths – i.e., for the backup to be sent directly to protection storage without going through another host – storage nodes are either not required at all or only required for negotiation of that data path.

It cannot be stressed enough that the most critical difference between other data protection methods discussed, and backup and recovery systems, is the *off-platform* component. By taking a completely independent copy of the data and storing it elsewhere under the control of a wholly different system, backup and recovery solutions act as a safety net for the data of the organization.

While systems with low RTOs and highly granular RPOs will typically need to include *on-platform* data recovery functionality (e.g., snapshots, replication, CDP), the importance of backup and recovery services in providing a robust and comprehensive ability to recover data within the business cannot be overstated.

2.4.4.2 How backup and recovery supports recoverability

Backup and recovery services within a business can support recovery through a variety of ways. Recall from Chapter 1, "Recovery Categories", that recovery types can be categorized as follows:

1. Operational
2. Long-term (compliance)
3. Disaster
4. Business continuity
5. Data re-use
6. Audit (test)

A backup and recovery environment can be used to accommodate all of these different recovery goals, thus providing a considerable boost to data recoverability within an environment.

It is common practice for backup and recovery to be used to assist with operational recovery. The most common backup schedule is for a data copy to be taken once every 24 hours; this might be a full backup (complete transfer of the selected data), incremental backup (transferring just the data that has changed since the last backup), differential backup (transferring the data that has changed since the last full or differential backup), or a synthetic backup (merging a new incremental with previous incremental/differential and full backups to create a new full backup). Regardless, this gives a RPO of a day, and the RTO will be dependent on configuration and technology performance. However, backups may be more frequent than this – database servers for instance may get backups every 15 minutes across a day to store their archived redo logs, ensuring off-platform protection of the logs that allow for highly granular database recovery.

We'll cover long-term/compliance recoveries in more detail in a later section; suffice it to say that there are two standard approaches to maintaining compliance data within a business:

1. **In workload**: In this scenario, workloads (e.g., databases) have 'never delete' policies. Data, added to the workload, is maintained indefinitely, or at least for any regulatory compliance period. If the data is purged at all, it is only purged after it is no longer legally required, which may be in the order of years or decades. In such an approach, there may be no need to retain long-term backups of the workload, since compliance data can be retrieved from any of the recent operational (e.g., daily) backups.
2. **In backup**: Not all applications and services are designed for long-term storage of compliance data. Even when they are, not all businesses can afford to keep that data online in high-performance storage platforms. This is where backup and recovery solutions come into play. In addition to daily backups for operational retention, a business can use *monthly* backups (typically, monthly *full* backups) to facilitate recovery of compliance data. Thus, retrieving a copy of a database, virtual machine, file, or other data is as simple as running a recovery in the same way you might recover from an overnight backup.

While there are pros and cons of both approaches, it's common to see a mix of the two used in an environment, since it's rare for *all* applications and services in a business to support compliance retention within their own workloads.

Backup and recovery systems can play a part in disaster recovery and business continuity processes as well. For smaller businesses, backup and recovery systems may *be* the DR/BC method used by the business. For larger businesses, there may be considerable reliance on on-platform protection methods (replication, snapshots, and CDP), *but* backup and recovery is a fallback solution in the event of a significant failure.

Recovery testing is common practice within backup environments, also. This may be for internal checking (e.g., when deploying a new workload, or random validation of backups), or for meeting audit compliance – proving that workloads the company has a legal obligation to protect are recoverable.

And finally, it is quite common to see backup and recovery solutions used to facilitate data re-use functions within an environment. There are three areas that attract particular attention:

1. **Repopulation of dev and test systems:** This refers to updating a development or test copy of a system with the latest copy of data from its production system (this is sometimes referred to as a *copy refresh*). Rather than copy the data directly from the production system, potentially resulting in a performance impact or even outage on the production system, data is recovered from the *backup* of the production system.

2. **Data warehousing and data lakes:** Similar to the above, if the business maintains a data warehouse or a data lake with a large pool of data contained within it, this pool can be updated by recovering production data from backups, rather than having to stream production data directly to the warehouse.

3. **Instant recovery:** Instant recovery, or instant access, is a feature offered by a number of backup and recovery services that use disk (as opposed to tape or object) for storing backups. Particularly useful in virtualisation environments (e.g., VMware), a read/write snapshot[1] of a virtual machine can be taken on the data protection storage, and temporarily presented to the hypervisor service via a network mount (e.g., network file system). This allows the hypervisor to immediately boot the virtual machine from that read/write snapshot and allow access to it within seconds. Advanced configurations will even allow the running virtual machine to be 'transitioned' across from the backup storage to the primary storage while it is running. This can be used for testing (e.g., finding out whether a proposed patch will work) or

high speed recoveries. While this can be done for workloads other than virtual machines, the virtual machine use-case is the most commonplace.

In short, backup and recovery solutions can significantly enhance the data and workload recoverability options available to a business.

2.5 RECOVERABILITY CONSIDERATIONS

2.5.1 Speed and service level agreements

Ultimately, we protect data so we can recover it if it is lost. So, the question is – how fast do you want to recover your data in the event of it being lost?

It's tempting (and common) for many businesses to just answer "immediately", but this comes with a cost. Instead, the desired recovery performance is typically balanced against the following metrics:

1. **Criticality of the data**: The more critical the data is to the business, the faster you'll want to recover it. Data sets and workloads that are deemed 'mission critical' will have the highest recovery speed requirements – you'll want to retrieve the backup as fast as you wrote it. For dev and test workloads, or secondary storage areas, you may be content with slower recovery speeds.
2. **When the data was protected**: Recovering data from last night's backup will usually have a much higher recovery speed requirement than recovering a compliance copy from several years ago.
3. **How it was backed up**: The way in which you backup data can affect the speed with which you can recover it. For instance, it's common to parallelize database backups – i.e., run multiple streams of data from the database to the data protection storage at the same time. The number of streams you use for backup often places a direct limit on the number of streams you can use for recovery. (E.g., if the database supports up to 32 parallel streams for backup, but you only use 16 for the backup, it's unlikely you'll be able to recover more than 16 streams simultaneously because only 16 discrete streams were *written* in the first place.)

4. **Where it was backed up**: Any storage platform you write backups to will impose limits (performance or cost) on reading from those backups. A cloud backup provider may be easy to setup but require you to pay to get your data back. Cold object archive storage may be cheap, but if you are forced to wait hours after initiating a recovery request before data starts streaming back, it may not allow you to meet service level agreements (SLAs) for the recovery of, say, last night's mission-critical database backup.

A sensible approach to determining required recovery speeds is to classify data and workloads within the organisation into different *tiers*. The number and name of data/workload tiers within a business will vary, of course, but common categorisations can be simple numeric values (e.g., Tier 1 being the highest criticality and Tier 4 being the lowest), or names based on precious metals (e.g., Platinum, Gold, Silver, and Bronze). Regardless of the nomenclature, the purpose here is to identify the criticality each dataset or workload represents to the business. Once these tiers are established, you can start to assign not only data protection (SLAs) to them, but also recovery targets, with recovery targets further refined by the age of the data.

The SLAs (or objectives, in many businesses) will include details of how much data can be lost (recovery *point* objective, or RPO) and how long it takes to recover the data (recovery *time* objective, or RTO). These RPOs and RTOs will also potentially have two flavours – one based on recovery from *on-platform* protection methods (e.g., snapshots) and one based on *off-platform* protection methods (e.g., backup and recovery services). Both should be defined, because there is always the risk that on-platform protection formats will either fail or fail to facilitate the retention period required for the recovery (Table 2.4).

When it comes to recovery from backup, the distinction between *operational recovery* (a recent backup) and *compliance recovery* (from a long-term retention backup) may seem sufficient, but does not necessarily always reflect reality within the business. Further distinctions may be useful when planning RTOs, in particular, based on the purpose of the recovery and the recency with which the backup was taken. For example, consider an operational retention of four weeks for a mission-critical database. Recovery objectives could conceivably shift along the following lines (Table 2.5):

Table 2.4 RTOs and RPOs per workload tier

	Platinum	Gold	Silver	Bronze
On-Platform RTO	Milliseconds/Zero for local copy (Synchronous Replication) Seconds for remote copy (Asynchronous Replication)	Seconds (CDP)	1 hour	N/A (Backup Only)
On-Platform RPO	Zero (no data loss)	Minutes	1 hour	24 hours
Backup (Operational) RTO	1 hour	4 hours	8 hours	7 days
Backup (Operational) RPO	15 minutes	8 hours	24 hours	24 hours
Backup (Compliance) RTO	5 business days	10 business days	None (No compliance retention)	None (No compliance retention)
Backup (Compliance) RPO	1 month for up to 7 years	1 month for up to 1 year	None (No compliance retention)	None (No compliance retention)

Table 2.5 Granular RTOs within the operational retention window

Age of backup	Recovery purpose	Recovery time objective
Under 48 hours	System disaster/service restoration	1 hour
2–7 Days	System disaster/service restoration	1–4 hours
Any age in operational retention	Data re-use (recover to dev/test system)	8–24 hours
Any age in operational retention	Audit	4–8 hours

It's important that both the business and IT help set RTOs and RPOs for service levels – at least for systems that support any critical or high-priority business function. The business teams will be able to provide direction on the criticality of the workload to overall business function and success; IT will be able to advise what *can* be achieved with either the technology at hand or budget available to meet those objectives. E.g., if recovering a 100 TB database from *backup*, it is important to have recovery objectives that can be met by the technology. While being able to recover that much data in, say, 1 hour might be desirable, a sustained throughput of 100 TB/hour will have a significantly higher cost than might be practicable.

The final consideration on recovery speed is the *impact* to other hosts and the network during the recovery process. Service providers for instance must provide appropriate guardrails for their environments to protect paying customers from *noisy neighbours* – other users of the service that use enough resources (CPU, memory, storage or network) that it impacts other subscribers on the same physical platforms. The *noisy neighbour* approach can play a factor within recoveries, too: while a high speed recovery that saturates LAN traffic may be acceptable for a dedicated, mission-critical service during a disaster recovery situation, such an impact may not be acceptable when the recovery is running just to populate a dev/test system for data re-use. Such considerations can be quite nuanced – a maximum speed/network saturation recovery may be OK *within* a datacentre, but running across datacentres over shared links used for inter-data-centre traffic may be unacceptable except in extreme emergencies.

2.5.2 Data format

The format of the recovered data can be an important consideration. For on-platform data protection (e.g., replication and snapshots), the data format will *almost* always be the same as the original data protected (there may be some exceptions possible with software-controlled protection and CDP). For off-platform protection, the actual recovery format may be significantly different from the backup format. Some examples are outlined below:

1. Virtual machine backups. If these are captured at the hypervisor level (i.e., backing up the virtual machine disks whole), data format options for recovery could include:
   a. Whole of virtual machine recovery (same data format)
   b. Individual or select virtual disk recovery (same data format, but reduced scope)
   c. Database recovery (database format recovery from an application-aware virtual machine backup)
   d. File level recovery, or FLR (recovery of individual files from protected virtual disks)

2. Block-based filesystem backups. These backups bypass the filesystem to perform a backup of the actual filesystem blocks, which can provide exceptional performance for dense filesystems. Data recovery formats include:
   a. Whole filesystem recovery (same data format)
   b. FLR (recovery of individual files from the block-based backup)
3. Database backups. Particularly for conventional Relational Database Management System (RDBMS) platforms (e.g., Oracle, Microsoft SQL), these will be generated in a specific database format. (Other database backups might be written as *exports*.) Data format options for recovery could include:
   a. Original database content (same data format)
   b. Database backup files (an alternate format that allows easy transfer of the data from one system to another, possibly version-independent)
   c. Exports (ASCII or UTF-8 ASCII format of the data, but usually only if this was the original backup format)
   d. Table or row-level content (a database format, but not necessarily the same as the original backup format)
   e. Data-masked (where the original data is restored in some usable format, but with certain sensitive information, such as credit card numbers or personally identifiable information, blanked out).

The data format for recovery also comes into play when recovering from long-term retention (compliance) backups, but in those cases, the question comes down to *compatibility*. We'll discuss this in more detail in Section 2.6.

2.5.3 Restore and recover model

Databases have long run with the concept of *restore* and *recover* as two different operations. In the world of databases, a *restore* typically refers to retrieving backup files from protection storage (disk, tape, etc.), whereupon a *recovery* operation can take place to use those restored files to bring the database back up to full operations. This will involve actions such as copying the restored files back into position (if they were restored to a staging location), then replaying log files to ensure the database is consistent and up to date to as close a point as possible as the failure.

This model can apply to more than just databases. In fact, in any situation where post-restore steps are required before a workload can be used again, there is an implicit *restore and recover* model operating.

Understanding when a two-step restore and recover method is important in determining what the *service restoration time* will be. It's easy to focus on RTO – how long does it take to complete the recovery process – as being solely based on the time it takes for data to stream from the backup storage system *to* the recovery target. If there are a number of post-restore operations required though before you can say the *service* has been restored, there are two very different recovery times – one being a subset of the other.

To ensure the difference between *recovery* and *service restoration* times are understood, you'll need to consider details such as:

- **How automatable is the recovery?** Post-restore operations can be automated in many circumstances, but they may also be more human/process driven. The inability to automate post-restore operations may introduce increased risk of human error, but taking the time to automate these steps correctly (and making sure all the *unhappy paths* are addressed) can be time-consuming.
- **What recovery types can be supported?** In essence, what are the resource requirements of the workload and the complexity of running it? Simple recoveries like individual files can be recovered in a variety of methods. However, multi-tera-byte databases might have different constraints. If a critical database requires 50 TB of storage, 512 GB of RAM, and 40 cores to run effectively, you may have fewer options regarding *where* you can recover it, even in test recovery scenarios.

2.5.4 Determining workload and recovery dependencies

Recall in Section 2.3, a view was established that you need to approach data protection with a view of the workloads and functions – the actual data you protect will follow as a natural consequence.

In Section 2.3, it was noted that multiple business functions might rely on similar workloads; within a vendor, for instance, *email* as a workload would be a dependency of a number of business functions including marketing, billing, supply-chain management, and internal communications.

As we move from recoveries of **data** to recoveries of **services**, it's critical to have a view of the web of dependencies between business services and workloads (and therefore, data) within the business. As the number of distinct business functions, and applications/workloads the business runs, increases the dependencies will increase in complexity. As you might appreciate, the increase in complexity merely makes it more critical that the dependencies are well understood.

System dependency *mapping* is the process where you construct views of:

- The workloads that business functions depend on
- The number of dependencies workloads have on them
- The number of other workloads a workload depends on

This data serves four essential purposes:

1. It allows you to comprehensively understand the disaster recovery requirements for a workload.
2. It allows you to comprehensively understand the IT aspects of business continuity requirements for a business function.
3. It allows you to establish recovery priorities in the event of a disaster or business continuity event.
4. It allows you to gain a better view of the required RTOs (and even at times RPOs) of complex systems with multiple interdependencies. For example, it may allow you to see scenarios where a critical system depends on a system which, if viewed in isolation, would be deemed low-priority for recoverability.

Dependency mapping can be done in a variety of ways, including diagrammatically and in tabular form (Table 2.6).

In the dependency mapping table, we can see there are four types of services:

- IT Infrastructure – Base level platform services
- IT Workloads – Workloads run by IT
- Business Workload – Workloads that exist solely to facilitate business services
- Business Functions – Actual functions performed by the business as part of its operations

Table 2.6 Tabular dependency mapping

Service	Service type	Depends on
1: Internet Access	IT Infrastructure	N/A
2: Network	IT Infrastructure	N/A
3: Storage	IT Infrastructure	2
4: Compute	IT Infrastructure	2, 3, 4
5: DNS	IT Workload	1, 2, 3, 4
6: Authentication	IT Workload	2, 3, 4, 5
7: File Services	Mixed Business/IT Workload	2, 3, 4, 5, 6
8: Virtualisation Services	IT Workload	2, 3, 4, 5, 6
9: Database Services	Business Workload	2, 3, 4, 5, 6, 8
10: Email Services	Mixed Business/IT Workload	1, 2, 3, 4, 5, 6, 8
11: Development Services	IT Workload	2, 3, 4, 5, 6, 8, 9
Customer Billing	Business Function	1, 2, 3, 4, 5, 6, 7, 8, 9, 10
Marketing	Business Function	1, 2, 3, 4, 5, 6, 7, 8, 10
Staff Payroll	Business Function	1, 2, 3, 4, 5, 6, 8, 9, 10

Once you map dependencies, you'll observe that they help to establish the *recovery order* in a critical incident. The base network infrastructure for instance is not dependent on any other IT infrastructure (though it's notable, particularly in on-premises environments, that it *does* depend on physical infrastructure such as facilities and power), yet is *depended upon* by every other IT workload, business workload, and business function. To simplify the mapping, you may decide to join multiple dependencies together – e.g., you might declare that storage, compute, and network are simply "Platform services".

As systems complexity increases, you may find benefits in doing nested dependencies – e.g., noting only first-order dependencies for any system or function and drawing up the dependencies in a way that shows the nesting. For example, you might say in our example table that Customer Billing has first-order dependencies of Database Services, File Services, and Email Services. Each of these services in turn has first-order dependencies, and so on.

You'll note though that the dependency mapping shown only goes as low as *services*; it doesn't attempt to identify individual hosts – the DNS service for instance may involve many servers running at strategic locations in the environment. This is not by mistake – a subsequent phase is to assign recovery profiles to the services outlined in the dependency maps, *then* assign SLAs (and appropriate data protection profiles) to the individual systems based on the services they provide.

2.5.5 Recovery SLA profiles

Before you can build out profiles for recovery SLAs, you must understand:

- What your data sets, workloads (services), and business functions are
- The criticality of the business functions and, by extension, the workloads and data sets that support those functions
- The dependencies between the business functions and workloads/ services

In Section 2.5.1, examples of SLAs covering RTOs and RPOs were provided. Once SLA profiles are established, they should be carried across to all workloads and data sets within the environment. While there will always be individual systems or data sets that do not exactly conform to a standard SLA, these should be the exception, rather than the rule.

Note that some businesses may refer to these as service level *objectives* rather than *agreements*, depending on how formal the process is between the business, IT, and any regulators that may impose requirements.

2.6 LONG-TERM RETENTION CONSIDERATIONS

Choosing to retain long-term (compliance) copies within backup and recovery solutions is a common (and valid) technique but does introduce challenges and special considerations that are often ignored. Many of the challenges specific to long-term retention only become more pronounced as the retention period grows. What is a (relatively) trivial problem to solve for a backup taken, say, 3 months ago becomes more difficult as the retention grows into multiple years and in some cases, decades.

Attaining *usable* recoveries from long-term backups is a three-sided challenge, encompassing data format, environment support, and non-functional support.

2.6.1 Historical data format drift

As alluded to earlier in Section 2.5.2, long-term retention can introduce particular challenges when it comes to data format. You might say that long-term retention focuses on the distinction: even if you *can* recover the data, can you *use* the data?

Some examples to consider here (that are by no means exhaustive) include:

1. **Virtual machine format**: Can the current version of your hypervisor platform still work with the virtual disk format from an image-based backup of a virtual machine from, say, 7 years ago?
2. **Database format**: Can the current version of your database platform still understand the database format that was in use when a backup was taken 7 years ago?
3. **Email format**: Can the current version of your email server platform still understand the storage format that was in use when a backup was taken 7 years ago?
4. **File format**: Can the current version of your *office platform* (e.g., word processing and spreadsheets) still understand the file format that was in use when a backup was taken 7 years ago? The problem can be even more foundational than this. Adobe introduced *Type 1* fonts in 1984, but finally retired support for their active use in new documents at the start of 2023. What happens if you can recover a document, but the lack of legacy font support means it can't be reliably opened?

2.6.2 Environment support

A challenge *before* you even reach consideration of data *formats* is the recovery *environment*. Are you even using the same database product today as you were when the long-term retention backup was taken? The same hypervisor? Has a workload you want to recover from 5 years ago been refactored from an on-premises architecture to something that now runs in-cloud? Has the workload been decommissioned entirely? What if the backup was written to tape and you don't actually have any tape drives any more to read it? Or what if the backup software has changed – not just version changes, but entirely different products and vendors?

All of these are real, tangible problems that businesses and their IT departments face when needing to recover from compliance backups. It is not unreasonable to suggest that many of these problems come from data protection being largely ignored, or treated as second-class citizen when it comes to planning and change-control within the business. However, while some problems do arise by lack of consideration for these potential challenges when making significant architectural changes within business systems, the other factor is a lack of forward planning in developing long-term retention strategies. In short: backups executed for operational recovery may not always be appropriate for long-term recovery. Rather than solving this at backup time, it is unfortunately all too common the case that environmental challenges like these are the proverbial can that gets kicked down the road for *someone else* to deal with. What happens then if that someone else is *you*?

To help *mitigate* this problem, you can make sure you keep a comprehensive archive of all old operating systems and software the business has used, for at least the duration of the long-term retention backups. You might also retain a record of all software licenses used. However, that can become problematic – to avoid issues with software piracy, many vendors require online validation of licenses. If an operating system has been deemed *out of service life* by its vendor by, say, 5 years, will the online activation service even work any longer?

If you store the operating system and application installers, will they even be valid on modern hardware? Or will legacy hardware platforms need to be maintained by the business? (You certainly want to avoid recovery procedures that start with, "Buy whatever compatible equipment you can from eBay".) Consider, for example, Apple's Macintosh platform. In 2006, Apple transitioned their Macintosh hardware platform from PowerPC CPUs to Intel CPUs. In 2020, they started transitioning the platform from Intel to a custom Advanced RISC Machine (ARM)-based architecture, instead. A business that has, say, a long-term retention policy for 20 years and has macOS backups must navigate not only the older versions of operating systems and applications, but potentially *two* CPU architecture transitions. Could you recover files from, say, a FileMaker

Pro backup taken on a PowerPC Macintosh to FileMaker Pro on an ARM Macintosh *and use the recovered data?*

This isn't a problem restricted to the Macintosh. Some businesses for instance might run their Oracle servers on AIX/Power platforms. Oracle, the company, often encourages customers running such platforms to switch across to their Exadata platform, which runs on Intel/X86 servers. The transition from AIX/Power to Intel/X86 results in an *endian* shift, which means backups taken on one platform would be gibberish if they could be recovered on the other. Businesses which retain long-term retention backups of their Oracle systems for compliance reasons cannot recover compliance AIX/Power Oracle backups directly to Intel/X86 – they would have to be recovered to a compatible AIX/Power system first, and then byte-translated before they could be run on an Exadata platform.

In short, you may find that *data format* and *environmental support* are intrinsically linked challenges.

2.6.3 Non-functional support

Non-functional support refers to items outside the purview of data format and environmental considerations. This can include:

1. **Software entitlement (support and maintenance):** Let's say that you have long-term retention backups of Oracle databases stored in some backup vendor X's software. Fast-forward 5 years – your business now uses vendor Y for backup software, and has transitioned from Oracle to PostgreSQL. Do you even have an *entitlement* to run either the old backup software or Oracle?
2. **Knowledge:** Repeating our prior example – let's assume you have (or can acquire) legal permission to use the prior backup software and Oracle. Assume as well you have the hardware platforms and operating systems necessary to restore that compliance database copy on to. Do you have any staff who have the knowledge required to execute a successful recovery? That question has to be asked of both the backup product *and* the recovered workload.

Non-functional support areas can represent a considerable cost if not managed in advance, particularly in situations where you have to recover data for legal compliance reasons – what happens, for instance, if the only way you can achieve the recovery is to rent equipment, purchase new software entitlements, and engage specialist contractors? How can you balance recoverability from long-term retention requirements with privacy and right-to-be-forgotten legislation (e.g., General Data Protection Regulation)?

2.6.4 Required capacity

In addition to data formats, environmental support, and non-functional support challenges introduced by long-term retention/compliance backups, one additional consideration is the amount of data storage required by them. If, for instance, you're keeping operational retention backups for 28 days, and monthly compliance backups for 7 years, the volume of data potentially stored by those compliance backups can significantly eclipse the operational retention. For instance, consider an environment that has a starting size of 500 TB of data and 10% annual growth. If we assume weekly full backups and daily incremental backups with a 3% daily change rate, the total *minimum* amount of data stored in operational backups at any one time will be:

- 4 × the current data set size
- 4 × 6 × 3% of the current data set size

So at the very start of the process, before any data growth has happened, an operational backup sequence would account for:

- 4 × 500 TB = 2,000 TB
- 24 × (3% of 500 TB) = 360 TB
- For a total of 2,360 TB

At the end of 7 years of continuous 10% year on year growth, the business data size will have grown to approximately 974 TB, resulting in a 'final' operational backup size of:

- 4 × 974 TB = 3,896 TB
- 24 × (3% of 974 TB) = 701.28 TB
- For a total of approximately 4,597 TB

On the other hand, 84 monthly backups with 10% annual growth will result in a long-term retention/compliance data set of approximately

59,961 TB – the long-term retention at the end of the 7 years will represent *13 times more data* than the operational retention at the same time.

While storage-efficient formats such as deduplication can help to reduce the actual occupied storage, the 'drift' in data over time means that deduplication can only help so much for long-term retention copies. Furthermore, *efficient* deduplication requires some level of interactive IO capability from the storage platform; deep archive storage (e.g., 'cold' archive object storage in public cloud) may not be sufficiently compatible with deduplication to deliver effective utilisation.

The net consideration here is: long-term retention backups can represent a significant amount of data to manage.

2.6.5 Best practice approaches to long-term retention backups

We'll close out this section by noting some best practice approaches you can take to optimise your chances of a successful recovery of *usable* data from long-term retention backups.

1. **Store only what you need:** This implies having a sufficient data classification process to understand what you *do* and *do not* need to keep for compliance reasons. "Keep it all" can be a costly decision. This can also mean avoiding having the same blanket long-term retention period for everything you keep for compliance purposes. Make sure the compliance requirements are tailored for each workload. That may require a little more upfront management but can significantly reduce the total amount of data stored.

2. **Delete it when it's no longer required:** Some companies keep their long-term retention data longer than they're legally required to, because it's seen as easier to manage than deleting. However, data retained is data that may be legally discovered. Long-term retention processes should always mitigate risk by deleting data when it is no longer legally required.

3. **Wherever possible, use neutral data formats:** You may struggle to entirely ameliorate data format and environment support issues, not to mention non-functional support challenges. However, if you take the time to make sure long-term retention backups are written in a neutral data format (even if

they're written in *both* the native and neutral data format), you'll give future IT staff within your organisation a better chance of dealing with compliance recoveries. A 7-year-old backup of an Oracle database may not be compatible with the current PostgreSQL platform, but a 7-year-old backup of an *export* of an Oracle database stands a better chance of a current database administrator being able to work out a way to make the data actively usable.

4. **Use archive where possible**: A valid approach to long-term retention of data is to store data you need to keep in an archive platform that meets records retention compliance requirements. This typically means a replicated storage platform with immutability. Once data has been transferred into the archive platform, it can be removed from both primary storage *and* backup operations. (The same caveats apply to archive platforms as we've mentioned here: make sure the data is stored in a neutral format that is not dependent on the application used to create it for access.)

5. **Evaluate where data can be retained in the original application**: Where archive is not possible, evaluate where data may be retained in the original application in a method which protects it from erasure or modification. Doing so will increase the amount of primary storage needed, but the net benefit is there will be no need for long-term retention backups for that workload; instead, standard operational backups will retain the compliance data.

6. **Evaluate where data lakes or warehouses can be used**: Where the data cannot be archived or retained in the original location, it may be possible to instead store the long-term retention data within a data lake, or data warehouse – again, so long as it can be stored in such a way that it is protected from erasure or modification. Like storing it within the original application, this means you can move away from long-term retention backups, since standard operational backups of the data lake/warehouse will include the compliance data.

If all of this seems complex or challenging, that's because it is! Long-term retention of backups is the proverbial "kicking the can down the road" exercise in most businesses; compliance requirements mean the data must be kept. Beyond that, dealing with the recovery is passed on to the schmucks who receive the recovery request sometimes years or decades later. There is essentially entrenched apathy in the industry that recovery from long-term retention backups is *someone else's problem*. But at some point, it will be *your problem*. So it's imperative you design the solution with such recoveries in mind at the time the backups are taken.

2.7 COMMON CHALLENGES

2.7.1 OS/application currency

All operating system and applications are versioned, and each version has a limited lifespan. This presents two distinct issues for data protection – currency and its lack thereof.

As a business engages in programs to update operating systems and applications to newer versions, making sure the data protection solution is compatible with those newer versions is essential to ensure ongoing recoverability of data. Yet, compatibility is not always guaranteed. After all, how can someone guarantee that their product, released in say, 2021, will be compatible with another product, released in 2023? Data protection solutions have their own currency and version lifecycle, and given the number of applications and operating systems available, it's not possible for data protection solutions to instantly release (or even instantly qualify) new versions of operating systems and applications as soon as they're released. Since the purpose of a data protection solution *is* recoverability of the data, qualification can involve rigorous testing. But rigorous testing is the bare minimum that is required here – when OS and application vendors release new features, or change their core architecture, data protection vendors must implement changes to *their* product to provide support. The engineering effort to make those changes must also be interwoven with efforts on feature enhancements and other market initiatives.

So, the takeaway for OS and application currency is: Don't forget to include data protection qualification (from the vendors, and your teams themselves) in your plans for updating software within your IT systems.

The other side of the currency coin is the lack of currency. Or we might say that the problem described above is *future currency*, and the other problem is *backward currency*. How long can, or should, data protection solutions support older versions of operating systems and applications? It's not at all uncommon to find situations where businesses evaluate and sign-off against the risk of running an operating system or application that has gone beyond *end of service life*, or where the original vendor *no longer exists*. Yet, having signed off against such a risk, there is then a demand that all their *current vendors* (including data protection) support such systems. This is a challenge you do not want to find yourself in – either as a business (end-customer or system integrator) or as a data protection vendor. Imagine, for instance, being required in 2023 to deliver a modern solution with deep storage efficiencies (e.g., client-side deduplication, full zero-trust security) that supports cloud solutions, modern applications, and operating systems – and some *critical service running on Microsoft NT4*. This idea becomes even more farcical when we consider data protection products that weren't released to market until *decades after* vendors ceased support of old operating systems and applications. If you think back to the challenges posed by long-term retention, you'll see that those same challenges exist in some form or another for data protection vendors as current IT solutions evolve. This means providing ongoing support for applications and operating systems that are sometimes decades beyond their service life is a costly, time-consuming, and even potentially risky process.

2.7.2 Security and privacy

There is a careful balance to tread between data protection, security, and privacy. A system put in place to protect data must be able to at least *read* that data. As the risk of cyber-attacks increase in businesses, data protection environments become an obvious target for both inflicting damage on the data at rest in the organization and exfiltrating of data. In such situations, privacy concerns also come to bear – data stolen from a data protection solution, particularly one keeping compliance records may even include data which the business was legally required to delete. While processes might be in place within the business to identify such data during recovery operations and reapply deletions, cyber-attackers who are intent on data exfiltration are unlikely to follow them.

With security teams becoming increasingly invested in IT decision-making processes, data protection solutions now get significantly heightened attention. The evolution of *zero trust* as a systems principle means that it is essential for data protection solutions to articulate with a high degree of granularity *exactly* what privileges they require for normal operations – and even *justify* those privileges when questioned. At times, this can make integration an even more fragile operation than before. Once carte blanche administration privileges are removed from data protection processes and granular access is defined, the system may become more secure, but it also may be more exposed to encountering deployment-by-deployment challenges based on *how* someone has configured security within their organization. That's not to say these problems shouldn't be fixed – highly granular security for data protection is the ideal approach. But it is important to recognize that it introduces complexity, too.

At a simpler, but immediately more noticeable level, auditing – or more precisely, *real-time auditing* – has become a mandatory feature for any enterprise data protection solution. Security teams tasked with identifying and fending off cyber-attacks, data exfiltration, and a myriad of other potentially costly and embarrassing situations rely first and foremost on accurate, immediate logging of critical activities within the IT systems of the business. Given the reach that data protection systems have, a minimum of recovery operations, deletions, and configuration changes all need to be logged as soon as they occur, and be logged to a system under the control of the security team.

The challenge posed by security within data protection is walking an increasingly fine line between addressing the security requirements for the business and the functional requirements for data protection. This is a challenge shared jointly by security and data protection teams, and requires as much if not more attention to process as it does to the technology being used.

2.7.3 Edge to core to cloud

An evolving catchphrase in the IT industry is "edge to core to cloud", representing where the three main pools of data for a business reside – within edge systems, within traditional datacentres, and within public clouds.

The data protection challenge posed by *edge to core to cloud* however is that each of these areas of the IT systems for a business generates considerably different protection and recoverability requirements.

Or, to simplify this: you're unlikely to find a single all-encompassing data protection solution that can meet all your data protection requirements at the edge, in the datacentre, and in the public cloud.

Consider, for instance, the traditional edge: desktops and laptops. These are systems that at any time might be switched off, or disconnected from the network – particularly *outside* of work hours. Yet traditional datacentre backup and recovery solutions are timed to take place *outside* of work hours. Laptops may be increasingly connected thanks to cellular tethering, but tethering is typically over *metered* networks. Traditional datacentre backup and recovery solutions work on the principle of getting as much data as possible across the network links in as short a time as possible – this approach, applied to a metered network, could have significant financial implications, not to mention interrupt the user's work.

More modern edge considerations such as servers deployed in hostile environments, sensors deployed at regular intervals inside water pipes, or trace element detection systems in sewerage processing systems can present even more challenging approaches to data recoverability. In most cases, the solution here is to focus in getting the required data back to a traditional datacentre and protecting it from there using traditional methods.

Within public cloud environments, things become potentially more complex – the differing functions and access levels between Infrastructure-as-a-Service (IaaS), Platform-as-a-Service (PaaS), and Software-as-a-Service (SaaS) each impose their own data protection challenges and considerations – and that's before we consider the myriad of other *as-a-Service* (aaS) offerings cloud providers regularly introduce to make their offerings more compelling. We'll discuss this further in Section 2.8.

To provide a comprehensive recoverability solution you'll find yourself needing to address edge, core, and cloud use cases. But you may have to accept you'll need to tailor what you do to the network and platform limitations imposed by each of those locations. Shoehorning all three platforms into a single methodology is almost guaranteed to cause you significant recoverability headaches.

2.7.4 Compliance

In terms of recoverability, there are three typical compliance considerations to watch out for within data protection architecture. These are:

- **Retention compliance:** Ensuring that you meet any externally imposed, or internally required, timeframes for recoverability of data protection copies.

- **Immutability compliance:** Ensuring that you meet any externally imposed, or internally required, restrictions on guaranteed inalterability of data protection copies.
- **Access compliance:** Ensuring that you meet any externally imposed, or internally required, security settings regarding *who* is authorised to recover from *which* data protection copies, and to *where* those recoveries can go.

All three of these are essential for ensuring:

- Your data remains unalterably recoverable for the required timeframe *and*
- Only the appropriately authorised people can recover it.

2.8 SPECIAL CONSIDERATIONS FOR PUBLIC CLOUD WORKLOADS

2.8.1 The elephant in the room

When discussing data resilience, recoverability, or protection as it relates to public cloud workloads, the most fundamental consideration is this: you are responsible for protecting your data.

"4.5 You are responsible for properly configuring and using the Services and taking your own steps to maintain appropriate security, protection and backup of your Services Content."

Digital Ocean Terms of Service Agreement, 5 February 2022, https://www.digitalocean.com/legal/terms-of-service-agreement

---

Regardless of which cloud provider you use, the message is the same: they store the data you pay them to store and run the services you pay them to run, but if something happens to that data, the only entity responsible and accountable for getting it back is *you*. It doesn't matter whether you're using Infrastructure-as-a-Service (IaaS), Platform-as-a-Service (PaaS), Software-as-a-Service (SaaS) – or any other of a myriad of any other cloud functions, making sure you have an avenue to recover that data is *your* responsibility. This even applies (largely) in situations where you use a public cloud *backup* provider. For instance, the end user license agreement for the SaaS backup provider Spanning states:

"Licensee agrees that, except for Spanning's gross negligence or willful [sic] misconduct, Spanning shall not be responsible or liable for the unauthorized access to, alteration of, or deletion, correction, destruction, corruption, damage, loss or failure to secure or store Customer Data. Licensee acknowledges and agrees that it bears sole responsibility for adequately controlling, processing, storing and backing up its Customer Data."

Spanning End User License Agreement, https://spanning.com/downloads/EULA.pdf

In short, even when you pay for data protection within the public cloud, the responsibility for making sure your data is protected still (by and large) resides with *you*.

Regardless of whether you are an IT professional or casual user of public cloud services, it is *critical* that you always remain mindful of this. Despite cloud services having existed now for decades, and the sheer pervasiveness of them in our professional and personal lives, it is breathtakingly astonishing how frequently people either forget or ignore the fact that cloud providers *are not responsible* for data protection.

As cloud services continue to be woven into business processes, they too must be accounted for in dependency tracking and mapping between systems, particularly since every cloud service you use will have differing SLAs. For instance, if a cloud provider only offers a 24-hour SLA for dealing with an issue on their platform, it would be difficult for the IT team to offer a 1-hour SLA for a workload that depends on the cloud platform. This isn't a new problem, as such, since it can occur within traditional datacentres using a mix of vendors and service providers – but the complexity does increase as cloud adoption increases.

2.8.2 Protection systems

There are four types of protection systems to be considered within the public cloud. These are: cloud provider, backup-as-a-Service, traditional, or export.

Like data protection methods discussed earlier in this chapter (replication, snapshots, backup and recovery, etc.), these systems are not *all-or-nothing*; while some businesses might go "all in" on a single method, as regulatory rigour is increasingly turning its attention to public cloud workloads, a hybrid approach to protection encompassing multiple systems is becoming increasingly common.

2.8.2.1 Cloud provider

The most common system you'll see used most in the public cloud comes from the cloud providers themselves. That is, businesses making use of AWS will make use of the options provided by AWS to protect data, those using Azure will make use of Azure data protection, and so on.

An obvious advantage of using the public cloud provider for data protection services is that they are likely to have the deepest hooks into their own systems. This is akin to backup and recovery services for hypervisors; modern protection of 'guest' systems can be optimized (at least in terms of speed) by working with the hypervisor by backing up the virtual machine containers rather than needing to deploy an agent within the virtual machine.

Particularly for the purposes of achieving *operational* recovery, this method can be appealing, but as public cloud environments grow, it can introduce management and cost complexities. For instance, a business may have dozens or even hundreds of accounts with a public cloud provider. Does the cloud provider's protection get configured and maintained across all accounts simultaneously, or does it need to be done within each account? This can raise traditional problems to be found with workgroup and end-user data protection solutions: visibility. How easy is it to see or understand your protection status across every account, simultaneously?

2.8.2.2 Backup-as-a-service

Another common system within the public cloud space is backup-as-a-service (BaaS). BaaS can be used either for cloud or on-premises workloads, though the level of support for workload types and locations will vary substantially from provider to provider.

BaaS providers often work using a SaaS-like model; you pay an ongoing subscription for access to the provider. You then link the provider to your workloads (e.g., give it secure connections to your public cloud accounts) and configure backup and recovery policies. The BaaS provider might egress your data as part of the protection process, or it might act as an umbrella management system against the standard cloud provider protection mechanisms (or a combination of the two).

One of the most common areas to see BaaS is in the protection of SaaS workloads. Within a SaaS environment, the cloud provider manages almost all aspects of the infrastructure stack for you, right up to and including the actual application you're using. You may get administrative access to a tenancy within that stack, but ultimately the only part of the solution you *own* is your data. This means solutions such as traditional backup and recovery agents have no location to be installed. Instead, this has opened the market to BaaS providers to develop custom software solutions to protect business data, even when there is no access to the rest of the infrastructure stack. Two of the most common SaaS data sets targeted by BaaS providers are Microsoft 365 and Salesforce. These products fill a crucial gap for subscribers – while SaaS providers ensure the overall service is operational, and are likely to have some regional recoverability capability, they are not in the business of providing robust tenant-level data recovery tools.

2.8.2.3 Traditional

Traditional data protection vendors have a role to play in cloud-based recoverability strategies, too, particularly when there are operational and cost advantages to maintaining similar data protection strategies on-premises and within the public cloud.

Data protection vendors that have spent decades honing storage efficiency (e.g., via deduplication) can offer cost savings, too. While virtual appliances may add some cost to compute resources within a public cloud, significant data reductions can offset this, particularly when looking at the storage of long-term retention backups.

But there is another reason why traditional data protection vendors can play a role in cloud-based recoverability, and that is *workload mobility*. If you're protecting data in a cloud provider using the systems provided by that provider, your data stays in their cloud. That's good for them, and it may be good for operational recovery, but what happens if your business needs to regularly use that data in another cloud provider, or even wants to move the workload permanently – either between cloud providers or repatriating part/all of the workload to an on-premises style location?

2.8.2.4 Export

We most commonly think of data *exports* when it comes to databases. While you can back up a proprietary database using tools or application programming interfaces (APIs) provided by the backup vendor, the resulting backup will be something that you can only restore to the original database vendor. For example, Microsoft SQL Server can't just recover an Oracle RMAN backup.

Workloads running in IaaS within the public cloud are relatively accessible because you have full access to the application running the data. However, there are cost and efficiency concerns with running a full infrastructure stack in the public cloud just to run, say, a PostgreSQL database server. This is where cloud *Platform-as-a-Service* models offer cost efficiencies – you can have the full flexibility of running a complex database service, without needing to administer the infrastructure required for the database.

Cloud providers invariably offer *some* mechanism for protecting PaaS workloads, often for more than just databases. However, that protection, as we mentioned before, is locked into the public cloud provider. For instance, AWS provides snapshot integration their Relational Database Service (RDS) platform. This allows subscribers to RDS hosted databases to take regular snapshots of their data for rapid operational recovery. But what happens if you need to keep compliance copies of that data, or work on a copy of the database elsewhere? While exports might often be considered "low tech", and not necessarily as efficient as other protection mechanisms, they should not be discounted from consideration depending on your requirements to achieve data recoverability. (Even if a cloud provider allows long-term retention of these snapshots, is it the most cost-effective way of doing so? What may be a question that can be ignored for short-term operational retention can grow to be a financial headache over years or decades.)

2.8.2.5 A hybrid model for data recoverability

Cloud-provider, BaaS, traditional backup and recovery, and export methods should not be considered as *all-or-nothing* approaches. A hybrid approach to data recoverability will suit the requirements of many businesses. For instance, let's consider a situation where you're running PostgreSQL via AWS's RDS solution, have Microsoft 365 for Office, Exchange and OneDrive storage, and have a regulatory compliance requirement to keep monthly copies of one of your key customer databases for 7 years. The regulator requires you to keep these compliance copies *on-site*. How might this be managed?

1. With Microsoft 365, your primary option will be leveraging a BaaS solution for this SaaS platform. (Legal hold, as an option within Microsoft 365, is not intended for backup and recovery services.)
2. For the databases running in AWS RDS, you'll need to make use of RDS snapshot technology to maintain operational recovery options; these snapshots can be used to execute fast recoveries in the event of a data corruption or deletion event.
3. For the compliance copies (monthly retention), you *could* keep long-term copies of your snapshots; AWS RDS for instance supports exporting database snapshots into Amazon S3. But this won't be *on-site*. Instead, you could orchestrate a process whereby:
   a. The last snapshot taken at the end of the month is restored.[2]
   b. Since the restored copy of the database isn't being used, it can be exported without risking data integrity issues in the exported stream.
   c. A regular virtual machine (e.g., a Linux EC2 instance) with a traditional backup product's filesystem agent software installed might be configured to connect to the recovered database and trigger an export, writing the export to local storage.
   d. Once the export is complete, the filesystem agent could be used to trigger a backup of the exported database files, writing the backup to deduplication storage.

2.8.3 Granular cost isn't free

Two of the significant appeals of the public cloud are:

- Rapid elasticity (provision or removal of services as required) and
- Consumption-based pricing

When considered together, the net result is *pay as you go* and *pay only for what you consume*. Yet data recoverability is something we often must consider not for days or weeks, but months, years, or decades. For example, consider a situation where you decide to

Table 2.7 Monthly Glacier-IR storage requirements and cost

Month	Total stored (TB)	Cost for month (USD)
I	100.797	412.86
2	202.399	829.03
3	304.810	1,248.50
4	408.038	1,671.32
5	512.089	2,095.52
6	616.970	2,527.11
7	722.687	2,960.13
8	829.247	3,396.60
9	936.657	3,386.55[a]
10	1,044.924	3,836.55
11	1,154.054	4,727.01
12	1,264.054	5,177.57

[a] Pricing calculations reveal a pricing tier inflection at approximately 900 TB stored, resulting in month 9 having a lower cost than month 8, despite storing more data.

store monthly backups for 7 years in AWS Glacier Instant Retrieval (IR). To minimize the cost of storage, you would compress the data before writing the monthly copy to Glacier IR each month. If the starting size (with compression) of your data were 100 TB, and your data (even with compression) featured 10% annual growth, you'd be looking at the first 12 months of data storage and cost[3] as shown in Table 2.7.

At the end of the first 12 months of operation, using month-by-month payment options only, you'd have paid a minimum of USD 32,268.75 for the service. (This does not capture any costs associated with putting the data into Glacier IR, which may come into play depending on how you achieve this compliance storage – but it has been left out for simplicity, since the amount transferred *in* each month will become progressively smaller, relatively, to the amount of data held in Glacier IR over the full 7 years.)

By the end of the 84th month, however, the monthly storage consumption will have grown to 11,992.293 TB – with a single month cost of USD 49,120.43 USD. The total cost paid over the 7 years will be approximately USD 1,868,148. (Again, that is before we consider any additional costs with the incremental trickling in of additional data each month.)

Cloud services are at times deceptively cheap. The cost profiles work most in your favour when you're not constantly increasing the amount of storage or compute you use. In a situation such as constantly growing long-term retention, your long-term spend can be predicted. To borrow a phrase from the gambling industry: the house always wins.

2.8.4 Service convenience, protection, and vendor lock-in

Public cloud services bring significant benefits to many businesses – most particularly, convenience. Yet, convenience isn't free. If your data is important to you, then the recoverability of that data should also be important to you.

Some public cloud providers will tout that they save businesses from vendor lock-in, as if it's something that only happens in on-premises environments. Cloud providers are, after all, vendors themselves. Yet, the simple truth is that if you don't plan your data options very carefully in the public cloud, you risk falling into not just vendor lock-in, but a data-hostage situation – where the cost of egress is higher than what the business can afford, but the only way to ensure the data doesn't get deleted is to keep paying those monthly fees.

When planning for data recoverability, look at simple, cheap, and flexible. You can only ever choose two, and no-where is this more pertinent than considering data recoverability in the public cloud.

 LESSON NINE: Public cloud doesn't eliminate the need for data resilient architecture. It just moves the work to a different location.

2.9 WRAPPING UP

When you consider data resilience in the business, the first and easiest mistake you can make is to approach it from the perspective of the *data*. Data is undoubtedly an important aspect of *data resilience*, but the data alone can't tell you anything about the level of resilience you need to achieve for it. Such understanding can only be achieved by having a clear picture of where the data fits into workloads and, by extension, business functions.

Or to put it another way: the business doesn't care so much about the data, but rather, what the data *enables* the business to do. That means your resilience planning has to understand what the business does with the data you're protecting.

NOTES

1   By presenting a read/write snapshot, the original backup remains unaltered, while the presented data can be manipulated as if it were live.
2   Restores from RDS snapshots, as of the time of writing, must always be to a different instance. Restoring the database to a different location is an essential part of this process.
3   Prices calculated from https://calculator.aws as of February 2023 for Glacier IR storage in US East (Ohio).

Chapter 3

Enabling recoverability

3.1 INTRODUCTION

In the previous chapter, we looked at techniques and considerations for data resilience. While data resilience by necessity includes *recovery*, the core focus is *avoiding* the recovery wherever possible. Recalling the FARR model for resilient workloads, there are four key aspects:

- Fault tolerance
- Availability
- Redundancy
- Recoverability

These four aspects are supported by a general principle of *robustness*.

But you'll note for those aspects, only one is about recoverability; the rest are about avoiding the need to recover data. In this chapter, we'll focus on various aspects of recovery environments and how/where they can help you.

Since this is about recoverability, much of the focus of this chapter concerns itself with backup and recovery solutions.

3.2 STORAGE TYPES

Recovering data means reading it from somewhere. Regardless of whether that's in the public cloud or a traditional on-premises location, there are three essential types of storage that you can consider for backup and recovery operations.

DOI: 10.1201/9781032624952-3

3.2.1 Tape

3.2.1.1 Overview

The oldest storage type for data backups that can still be found in operation is tape technology. While the early years of the industry saw a plethora of different tape formats (e.g., Reel to Reel, Digital Audio Tape (DAT) and Digital Data Storage (DDS), Quarter Inch Cartridge (QIC), Digital Linear Tape (DLT), and SuperDLT), the open systems industry has largely standardised on the Linear Tape Open (LTO) format, with the most recent generation, LTO-9, entering general availability in September 2021.

A typical tape storage system consists of three components:

- The tape cartridges (media)
- The tape drives, and
- A tape library (robot for moving tapes between storage slots and drives)

While smaller systems might consist of individual tape drives that require a human operator to load and unload tapes (sometimes referred to as a 'protein-based autoloader'), most businesses making use of tape will use a library with preferably two or more tape drives and a robot arm to automate media movement. Such libraries can provide nearline storage via slots for anywhere from a handful to hundreds, or thousands of tapes – all in reach of the robot arm(s) within the library.

Tape media stores a relatively large amount of data in a small physical space; an LTO-9 tape cartridge will store 18 TB of data uncompressed. Tape drives feature hardware compression systems – LTO-9 states a compression ratio of 2.5:1, meaning an 18 TB tape could theoretically hold up to 45 TB, though this is dependent on the data being written. (For example, sparsely populated virtual machines might achieve a compression ratio of 4:1 or higher, but pre-compressed multimedia or medical imaging files, or pre-encrypted data, would typically yield no additional compression at all on tape.)

Individual tape formats and drives are often rated at a high *streaming* speed, which refers to the speed at which the physical tape is passed over the heads in the drive. This equates to a MB/s rating – for instance, LTO-9 is rated at 400 MB/s uncompressed and 1000 MB/s compressed. *However*, when used as backup targets tapes are notorious at not handling gaps in data streams well. If the data being received falls below an optimum threshold for continuous writing, this can result in the tape drive having to bring the tape to a halt, then rewind it before starting to write again. Such a process is referred to as *shoe-shining*, and while modern tape drives have introduced buffers and speed-stepping to help overcome this, the problem persists, particularly when the operating environment cannot keep up with the native speed of the tape drive(s). (For instance, LTO-9 is rated at 400 MB/s uncompressed. So if an LTO-9 tape drive is attached to a backup server that only has a 1 Gbit connection to the systems it is protecting, shoe-shining will likely be a constant factor of the environment.)

Tape systems can come in two varieties – physical (traditional) or virtual. A virtual tape solution emulates all aspects of a physical tape solution, but can be run on more platforms, including the public cloud.

3.2.1.2 How does tape aid recoverability?

Tape offers two primary items that businesses may consider relevant to recoverability within their environments:

- 'Countably infinite' storage
- Offline storage

A disk storage system has a number of slots that can house the drives. Each drive in a slot participates in some way to the storage pool (as a data storage drive, parity drive, a hybrid of the two, or a spare). But in order to participate in that storage pool, the drives by necessity have to be *in* the storage array. A dense storage array might fit 60+ 3.5" drives in a space of 5 rack units (RU), meaning you could have 480 hard drives (HDD) or more within a standard 42 RU rack. But once the drives and the rack are full, the only option you have to increase capacity is to add another rack.

Tape media though is made to be removable. A tape library that fully occupies a single rack, holding a number of tape drives and potentially hundreds of tapes, does not have the same boundary problem that a disk array has. If all the tapes in the library are filled, they can be removed and replaced with empty tapes. (While this is not 'infinite' storage, we can draw a parallel to 'countably infinite' because the total storage pool can continue to increase, even if the percentage of the written storage pool that is immediately accessible at any time decreases.)

Organisations that need to write to storage without conventional bounds (e.g., particle accelerators such as CERN can generate 15+ PB of data per day[1]) may find that they have no alternative *but* to use tape to achieve their recoverability storage needs. Note though that the emphasis is on the *storage*, not necessarily the recoverability *performance*. No matter how you're storing data, retrieving 15 PB is going to be a time-consuming process.

Once tapes are removed from a tape drive (in a standalone configuration) or library, they are *offline*. They can be held for days, months, or years outside of the tape operation system. For businesses that are concerned with immutability, this is often seen as a cheap win. However, it is not without its risks – the quoted shelf life for tapes is based on strict environmental controls and handling; dropping a tape or exposing it to rapid temperature or humidity changes can cause degradation or even failure. The data stored on offline tapes, being inaccessible, is also unavailable for data reuse situations, such as scanning for anomalies or malware, or using for recoveries into dev/test environments – any time the data needs to be used, the tape must be loaded back into a system. It's also worth noting that tapes being offline means that if you need to recover from them, you can't recover immediately – the tape has to be loaded into a tape drive so that data can be read from it. This operation may take a minute or two if the tape is in the library and a tape drive is free. But it may take several hours (or more) if the tape has been removed from the tape library and sent off-site for storage. The time required to recall tapes from offsite need to be considered in SLAs and recovery point/time objectives unless you can guarantee that you always have an on-site copy of the tape and have a high probability of having tape drives available for recoveries.

While tape can help with recoverability, there are limitations imposed by its physical nature that can sometimes be a hindrance. Unlike disk that supports sequential and random operations, tape can only be used at any time for *either* sequential reading *or* sequential writing. That is, you cannot simultaneously read from and write to the same tape cartridge, and random IO operations spread over the entire capacity of the tape are not feasible for most use cases, even using the Linear Tape File System (LTFS) overlay available on modern LTO media. This means that if you want to conduct *mass recoveries* within your environment, you will likely need potentially even more tape drives than were used for backup, and a recovery distribution that can utilise as many tapes as you have tape drives at any time.

While virtual tape systems can overcome some of the recovery limitations posed by physical tape systems (e.g., you can provision a lot more virtual tape drives than may be feasible with physical tape drives), key operational elements of tape remain the same, regardless of whether they're virtual or physical – for example, you cannot concurrently read from and write to the same virtual tape.

3.2.2 Hard disk drives

3.2.2.1 Overview

Hard disk drives were first introduced in 1956; while they started as physical monsters with (compared to current standards) miniscule data storage space, these days they offer considerable storage space in a relatively small form factor.

By 2022, Western Digital had introduced a 26 TB 3.5" harddrive,[2] and special/niche use-case solid state drives (SSD) are available at capacities of 100 TB,[3] though SSD/flash storage in enterprise systems is currently more likely to top out at around 20 TB.

While a tape cartridge may offer more capacity than the average deployed disk, disk drives provide full random IO with seek times orders of magnitude faster than tape seek operations, and can handle multiple concurrent read/write operations, which is where they become interesting for data recoverability.

3.2.2.2 How does disk aid recoverability?

Both conventional HDD and SSD/flash storage can play a part in data recoverability.

If a primary storage platform uses flash-based storage, flash itself is essential for snapshots to avoid performance degradation.[4] But flash storage can also be useful in backup and recovery solutions, particularly for mission-critical systems that demand the highest possible performance when running a recovery, though in such situations the ability for networks to stream the data at the required speed and the receiving (recovering) system to *receive* the data at flash-read speed can be a limiting factor.

HDD-based storage usually offers a better $/GB storage cost profile than SSD/flash, making it more appealing for backup storage for most organisations. HDD storage systems have a performance profile that can be an order of magnitude (or more) lower than SSD/flash storage systems, but like their faster counterparts, introduce a few key attributes to support recoverability:

- Random IO
- Concurrent operations
- Online access

The ability to facilitate random IO is critical in most recovery scenarios. While some recoveries might require tens or more terabytes of data to be streamed retrieved from a single backup, many recoveries are much smaller in nature – a user has lost a file, a small virtual machine became corrupted, or a database administrator wants to retrieve a recent copy of a production database from backup.

The second factor introduced by disk-based storage is concurrent operations – this can refer to multiple concurrent reads, multiple concurrent writes, or a mix of both. If you have a tape-based recovery environment with four tape drives (all writing backups) and receive a recovery request, your only options are to either queue the recovery to start once a tape drive has been freed from backup operations or abort a backup to force the tape drive to become available for recoveries. With disk-based recovery solutions, you can start a recovery while backups are still running. Likewise, if you're using a tape for a recovery, but then need to start another recovery that needs the *same* tape, the only way you can facilitate simultaneous recovery is if the data in the second recovery request appears at some physical point after the current location of the tape to the tape heads. (Even then it is not guaranteed to be simultaneous – it just removes the risk of having to rewind the tape after the first recovery is complete.)

Finally, disk-based backups are online, and therefore immediately available for recovery purposes. While it could potentially take hours (or longer) for a recovery to start from an offline tape, most recoveries from disk can start in seconds. This also means disk-based backups are available for data re-use, anomaly detection, and so on.

Disk-based storage for recovery still has obvious limitations – there will always be some limit on the number of drives you can allocate to a single storage pool, placing an upper limit on the amount of storage you can write to (and therefore recover from). This can create additional management overheads for multiple pools of data. One solution to this that we'll cover further in this chapter is *deduplication*.

3.2.3 Object storage

3.2.3.1 Overview

Object storage was developed in the late 1990s as an alternative to traditional disk-based storage strategies (filesystem and block storage). Object storage allows data and rich levels of metadata to be stored without any consideration to the backing storage layout; instead, every object stored has a unique identifier associated with it, and objects may be subsequently retrieved by requesting that identifier.

Object storage is typically seen as being something offered by public cloud services (e.g., AWS S3 and Azure Blob), but it does not have to run within the public cloud. In fact, some of the earliest commercial applications of object storage were in on-premises archive platforms.

Object storage platforms can significantly exceed the sizes offered by traditional block and file storage systems. While file and block systems typically use RAID to provide fault tolerance in the event of drive failures, object storage typically uses erasure coding. Erasure coding, as an architecture, allows for data and parity fragments to be stored across drives regardless of whether they're in the same storage enclosure, rack, or even datacentre.

3.2.3.2 How does object storage aid recoverability?

You'll recall one of the ways tape aids recoverability is that it allows for 'countably infinite' storage; you can keep on increasing the size of the storage pool relative to the physical occupancy of the datacentre components used to house the online part of the storage pool.

Object storage offers a similar option for 'countably infinite' storage; AWS for instance do not state a limit to the size of the object storage pool you can write to, even if they place limits on the individual objects that you can write (5 TB[5]). This means that if you need to facilitate recovery from an extremely large pool of data (e.g., hundreds or thousands of petabytes), an object storage platform may support your requirements. Depending on the service tier of the platform, this may even be *online* storage, as opposed to tape's *offline* basis.

While object storage may offer similar boundless expansion like tape, it doesn't come without cost. There is of course a literal aspect to that cost – regardless of whether you're operating in a public cloud space or using on-premises object storage. But more than that, the nature of object storage makes it architecturally well suited for random, granular IO access rather than transactional throughput. That is, rather than focusing performance on allowing a single data stream to read at hundreds of megabytes or gigabytes per second, object storage's architecture is best suited for situations where thousands or more concurrent accesses are performed against relatively small units of data. Recovery systems require significant parallelisation in order to render high performance out of object storage platforms, and this may not always be guaranteed – particularly in a public cloud environment where cloud providers use controls to prevent 'noisy neighbours' from leaving other subscribers with a poor experience.

One area where object storage is gaining considerable popularity is for the storage of long-term retention/compliance data. Depending on the performance tier used, this may offer a significantly low price per GB per month for storage – though as we saw in Section 2.8.3 this is not necessarily an insubstantial cost. This can sometimes result in hybrid backup and recovery solutions that use more traditional disk drive-based storage for short-term (operational) retention and offload older copies of backups to object storage for bulk, cheap (comparatively) long-term recovery storage.

3.3 EFFICIENCY CONSIDERATIONS

3.3.1 Compression

3.3.1.1 Overview

For almost as long as we've been storing data, we've been seeking ways to reduce the amount of storage we need for it. There are two primary modes of compression: lossy and lossless. Lossy compression is used for some multimedia formats; such compression throws away data, irreversibly changing the nature of the data, but in a way that should keep the overall data meaningful to the observer. Such compression can be used to store digital video and photographs in much smaller space than their 'original' size – but once applied, cannot be undone.

Lossy compression is undesirable when it comes to data recovery situations. For instance, applying a 'compression' filter of throwing away every third banking transaction when backing up database log files for a financial institution's primary database is not in any way a desirable method of data reduction, since that content is irretrievably lost.

Lossless compression on the other hand focuses on reversible data reduction. In essence, it replaces repeated patterns in data files with pointers to a single copy of that data. Compression can be used for storage, and for transmission. For instance, WAN accelerators work by applying compression before data is sent over a WAN, thereby reducing the amount of data that needs to be sent, and helping to make up for lower bandwidth connections.

3.3.1.2 How does compression aid recoverability?

Compression can aid recoverability in a few different ways. These can include increases to backup performance, backup storage, and recovery performance.

If you can compress a data stream before you send it to be stored, you can reduce the amount of time it takes to complete the backup. A common concern here is that this may have a deleterious effect on the CPU utilisation of the host sending the data. While this is a valid concern, the CPU/memory impact of compressing data before sending it is usually *lower* than the system impact of handling all the additional network traffic. (This however may not hold true in situations where you are using agent-based software within virtual machine farms and backing up many virtual machines from the same physical server simultaneously.)

If we compress data before it is written to backup storage, we are likely able to increase the number of copies we're able to store on any given storage platform.[6] By virtue of holding more backup copies, we have more flexibility in recovering from data loss situations across a longer time.

When running a recovery, a key performance consideration is how long it takes to get the data from the backup storage (source) to the recovery host (target). If this is over a network connection, the bandwidth and congestion on the network can often become a limiting factor. If we can compress the data stream as it is read from the source storage, and transmit only the compressed data across to the target, we may be able to speed up the recovery. This may require additional CPU and memory consumption for recovery operations on the target, but if that system would otherwise be sitting idle without the recovered data, it may be an acceptable performance impact. (For example, transferring 5 TB of data across a 10 Gbit link would take at least 1 hour, 6 minutes, and 40 seconds. On the other hand, if the data could be compressed before transmission with a 3:1 compression ratio, the transfer could take less than 23 minutes.)

3.3.2 Deduplication

3.3.2.1 Overview

At its core, deduplication is a special form of compression. When we think of compression, we typically compress things like a data stream, a file, or a collection of files.

You might think of deduplication as *global* compression (for varying values of 'global'). For instance, consider the humble zip file. If you take a backup of your 'Documents' folder today by creating a zip file and storing it on an external drive with a dated filename (e.g., YYYY-MM-DD.zip), you'll be writing a compressed copy of your data. If you create a *new* zip file tomorrow of the same folder, placing it alongside yesterday's zip file, each of the two zip files will be compressed, but they won't be compressed *against each other*. To be precise, they will not be 'globally' compressed.

To better understand the impact of deduplication, let's consider the first two sentences of Jane Austin's *Pride and Prejudice*:

It is a truth universally acknowledged, that a single man in possession of a good fortune must be in want of a wife.

However little known the feelings or views of such a man may be on his first entering a neighbourhood, this truth is so well fixed in the minds of the surrounding families, that he is considered as the rightful property of some one or other of their daughters.

Deduplication can perform either fixed segment analysis (chunking data in specific byte sizes) or variable segment analysis (chunking data in different sizes based on 'logical' breaks in the data stream).

Fixed segment analysis can reduce processing time, but increase storage consumption, particularly in data sets that have inserts or modifications. Variable segment analysis may require additional processing time, but can often result in the best possible storage reduction. The size of the data segments can vary significantly between deduplication technologies – a good, efficient size averages at the 8 KB point, but less efficient techniques can go as high as 256 KB or 512 KB, which usually result in savings more akin to standard compression.

For our *Pride and Prejudice* example, we'll imagine variable segment analysis using word boundaries as the segment division markers. (For convenience, we'll ignore punctuation – obviously real-world deduplication would not, as there is no benefit to lossy deduplication.)

Figure 3.1 shows the first two sentences of *Pride and Prejudice*, with word-level segmentation. Now, let's consider a first backup of the text – which, if all you were doing were compression, is shown in Figure 3.2.

In Figure 3.2, all common words have been replaced by primitive hashes that are stored separately in a metadata store. Where the words appear in the original text, the hashes are instead referenced. (The actual mechanics of hashes and pointers to hashes will vary depending on implementation.)

If all we were doing were compression, Figure 3.2 might be an accurate representation. However, as mentioned previously, deduplication is *global*. That is, we expect that other backups, done later,

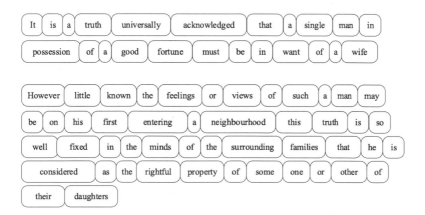

Figure 3.1 Start of *Pride and Prejudice*.

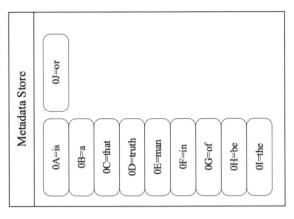

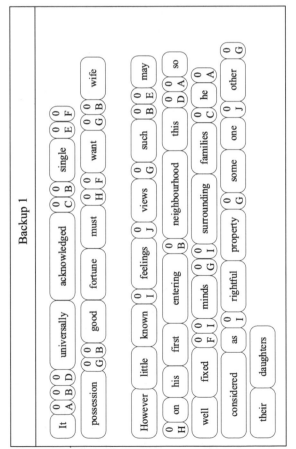

Figure 3.2 First backup of start of *Pride and Prejudice*.

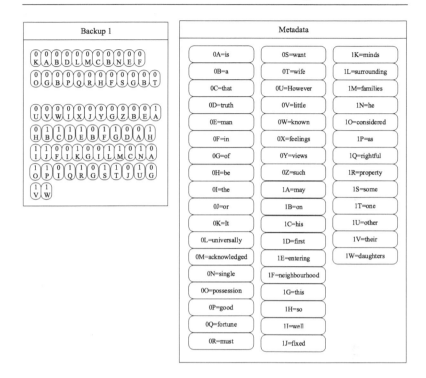

Figure 3.3 First deduplication backup of start of *Pride and Prejudice*.

will be stored in the same deduplication pool. The net effect is that all segments, regardless of whether they were unique in the data stream or not, will be stored according to a hashed identifier. So, that first backup might look more like Figure 3.3.

Deduplication can create capacity savings even in a single backup, depending on repeated content within that backup – but on just one backup, the capacity savings will more resemble compression algorithms. The true space saving comes from being able to perform deduplication against additional backups, i.e., across the entire global storage pool that is being used. Thus, when we do our second backup, we get a view such as that in Figure 3.4.

In this example, because we've backed up exactly the same content twice, all the metadata we needed to create to store the first backup can also be used to store the second backup, resulting in a near-100% capacity reduction. (Additional metadata identifying each backup and the *sequence* of segments within the backup would also come into play, hence *near*-100%.)

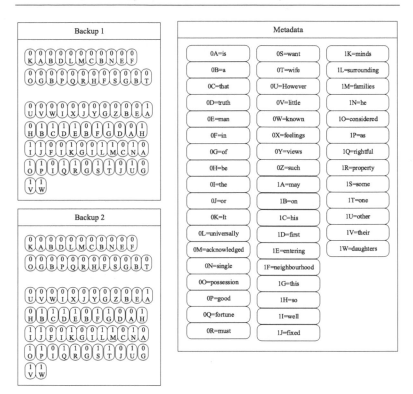

Figure 3.4 Two deduplicated backups of the start of *Pride and Prejudice*.

Deduplication is often paired with compression for further saving; all we've shown in the example is deduplicating the words. Within a deduplication storage pool you would typically also see the deduplicated data subsequently compressed, saving even more space.

While our example is not ideal (in some cases the metadata hash is bigger than the original data), it does serve to explain the difference between compression and deduplication – and highlight some of the primary benefits that deduplication can bring to a data protection environment.

To get the maximum benefit of deduplication, you'll want a large deduplication storage pool (the more data you can deduplicate against, the better chance you have of finding commonality) and relatively small data segmentation sizes. (8 KB segmentation sizes for instance strike an extremely effective balance between data reduction and metadata requirements.)

3.3.2.2 How does deduplication aid recoverability?

There are two ways in which deduplication aids recoverability:

- Increased number of copies held online
- Increased backup throughput

When disk storage first started to appear in backup and recovery solutions, it was used as a staging area. This was the time referred to as 'disk to disk to tape'; to avoid shoe-shining issues previously discussed, a pool of (usually cheap) disk-based storage was allocated to a backup server. The overnight backups would read from disk on client systems and write to the disk storage. Once the backups were complete, the backups would be moved from disk on the backup server to tape directly attached to the backup server. By transferring as a local read and write from large data files, shoe-shining could be avoided, and the data could get to tape faster. This could be used for a local copy and a remote copy (i.e., copy it to tape twice, with one tape to be kept off-site and one to be kept on-site). The side benefit created by this method was that if someone wanted to recover from the overnight backup, they could recover directly from disk rather than worrying about recalling, loading, and scanning through tapes.

However, because the backups were stored without any efficiency (usually even without compression, since that would then interfere with tape compression), they consumed a lot of space. If your biggest daily backup (e.g., your weekly full) was 10 TB, you needed at least 10 TB of disk to store the backup, and if you only had 10 TB of disk to store the backup, as soon as you finished copying it to tape you had to delete it to free up room for the next night's backup.

Deduplication was introduced to solve that specific problem – by deduplicating the data as it is written, less storage is needed to hold the backups, which means *more* copies can be stored. In a minimally ideal configuration, deduplication allows you to store *all* of your operational retention (e.g., 4 weeks of daily backups) in a usable capacity footprint the same size or even less than the original data requires.

By storing more copies of your backups online, you can run recoveries more easily (no need to wait for a tape drive to be free) and service more recovery points (different backups).

The second way deduplication aids recoverability is in increasing backup speed. There are two types of deduplication: source and target. It is specifically source-based deduplication that increases backup speed. Source-based deduplication has the deduplication API embedded into the backup client software. As the data is read for backup, the deduplication API does the initial segment processing and hashing against the data. As it reads and hashes the segments of data, it queries the deduplication storage to see if it has already stored that data. If it has, the deduplication storage creates another pointer to the originally stored data and the deduplicated backup throws the data away without transmitting it. Only data deemed to be unique is transmitted to the deduplication storage system (and usually compressed before sending). In our *Pride and Prejudice* example, this may not seem all that efficient. However, imagine a system averaging 8 KB segment sizes – each segment may require a hash as small as 20–32 bytes. In such a situation, it is far faster to transmit a query, "do you have data represented by 20 hundred bytes", and receive a response, than it is to transmit the full 8 KB. (An obvious side-effect of this is that the *first* backup of new data, particularly to an *empty* deduplication storage platform, can take longer.)

By increasing backup speed, we can also create more recovery points, as we have to transmit less data, and in doing so we can get our data *off-platform* faster, decreasing the amount of time in which you only have on-platform copies of your data.

When planning recoverability with deduplication, it is worth keeping in mind that the act of *rehydrating* the data can take time to complete. Ideally, this rehydration is done inline, as the data is read. But to read it quickly, the deduplication metadata store needs to be kept (as much as possible) in RAM, or on NVMe/SSD storage. It's also worth keeping in mind that source-based deduplication can save you from having to upgrade your core networking in your datacentres – e.g., with source-based deduplication, you may be able to continue to operate your datacentres on 10 Gbit networks, rather than increasing to 25 Gbit or higher – after all, the *biggest* data transfers you'll normally do are during backups.

Deduplicated recoveries however aren't a thing: you must transfer the data back, which consumes network bandwidth. Intelligent deduplication systems can help mitigate this (and therefore speed up recoveries) by compressing the data before sending it to the requesting host. The logic here is simple: if you need to recover a 100 TB database, and the database server is not operational until the database is restored, is it better to take 1333 minutes to transfer 100 TB (over a 10 Gbit link), or 666 minutes to transfer the data at a 2:1 compression (50 TB) over that same link? The additional CPU overhead to handle compression and decompression will be inconsequential compared to the time saved to achieve the recovery. While not guaranteed, deduplication *can* increase recovery speed. If metadata (i.e., deduplication pointers) is stored either in RAM or on NVMe/Flash storage, and the deduplication storage is spread over a large number of drives (flash or HDD), multi-stream restores can be massively parallelised, resulting in high speed throughput.

3.3.3 Single-instance storage

3.3.3.1 Overview

Single-instance storage is primarily associated with archive platforms, but it can also be used in primary storage and as a primitive form of deduplication in backup systems storage. You might think of single-instance storage as akin to the word-level deduplication example given in the previous section, but instead of storing single instances of data based on words, we store single instances of data based on documents (e.g., word processing files, spreadsheets, presentations, PDFs, emails, CAD files).

3.3.3.2 How does single-instance storage aid recoverability?

One of the best ways that single-instance storage aids in recoverability is by reducing the amount of data we need to protect. That is, when used in properly architected archive platforms.

A truly robust archive platform will use single-instancing to reduce the amount of data that needs to be stored. Additionally, data will be written to immutable storage (write once, read many, content locked for a defined period of time – or forever) and then replicated to immutable storage in another location. With the data unable to be deleted from the archive platform, and the archive platform itself protected from failure by a secondary copy in a separate physical location, it is safe to *remove* archived data from the backup process entirely.

By removing data that is safely archived from backup consideration, we leave backup storage requirements focused on just the data that needs to be protected, and we also reduce the amount of time it takes to complete backups, as we don't have to read as much data. This has a net-positive impact on recoverability within the environment. Additionally, archive platforms are typically complemented by powerful tagging and search capabilities, ensuring that archived data is easily discoverable, and therefore also easily recoverable. Where supported by application services (e.g., medical imaging systems often utilise archiving methodologies), we can also see the elimination of the need to use backups for long-term retention (compliance) copies.

3.3.4 Image-based backups

3.3.4.1 Overview

Image-based backups are used primarily in two different scenarios:

- For virtual machines (hypervisor-based protection) and
- For filesystems (block-based backup)

When open-systems virtualisation was first introduced to the datacentre, the traditional way to backup virtual machines was to install backup agent software within the virtual machine, as if it were a physical server. While this logically made sense, it could cause significant resource issues within the hypervisor environment. Virtualisation works because most virtual machines use only a small percentage of the resources they have available to them (memory, CPU, and IOPS); thus, many virtual machines can share resources on the same physical server. However, backups are designed for the purpose of moving data from the source system to the backup storage as fast as possible. When traditional, agent-based backups are started on every guest virtual machine on the same physical server, it can cause such a degree of resource contention that the systems become unusable.

Image-based backups of virtual machines work by having the backup software engage at the hypervisor level, rather than the per-virtual machine level. Typically this process works by taking a snapshot of the virtual machine, then backing up the container files that host the virtual machine, and releasing the snapshot. While there are variations on this process, the important factor is that rather than reading each file stored in the guest system as if it were a physical server, just a few large files are read from the hypervisor for each guest system.

Block-based backups of filesystems are another form of image-based backup. This technique is designed to overcome typical operating system limitations in walking (scanning) a dense filesystem.

In essence, a 10 TB filesystem comprising 10,000 × 1 GB files is significantly faster to backup than a 10 TB filesystem comprising 10,000,000 × 1 MB files, or worse yet, a 10 TB filesystem comprising 10,000,000,000 × 1 KB files. This rarely has anything to do with the backup software being used – rather, filesystem structures take more time to traverse sequentially as the number of files increases. A block-based backup avoids traversal times introduced by density by reading the blocks from the underlying *storage volume* that provides the filesystem, rather than walking the filesystem. (To prevent reading data that results in a corrupt backup image, or write-locking the filesystem during backup, this technique is typically coupled with volume snapshots – similar to the virtual machine technique previously described, a snapshot is taken of the volume and the backup is done against the snapshot.)

3.3.4.2 How do image-based backups aid recoverability?

Image-based backups primarily aid recoverability by allowing for more resource-efficient and faster backups. Regardless of whether the backup is of a virtual machine or a filesystem, an image-based backup may scan the same amount of data (or even more if virtual machine has been fully provisioned, or the occupied filesystem is much smaller than the available volume size), but that scanning process is a continuous stream of data rather than the haphazard stop/start nature of walking filesystems. When image-based backups are combined with deduplication, the risk of backing up *more* data than the 'raw' content is eliminated, and when combined with source-side deduplication, the amount of data transmitted is largely the same as if it were a traditional backup.

Additionally, by having the hypervisor coordinate the data transfer, rather than potentially having all guests simultaneously trying to send their data, the system load is lessened and resources are more effectively used.

As we've noted in previous sections, by providing mechanisms to speed up the backup, we're able to create more recovery points in the same amount of time, or get the off-platform copy of our data sooner – and both of these results aid recoverability.

It should be noted that while image-based backups offer the previously stated benefits for recoverability, they are not without their downsides. Image-based backups retained for *compliance* retention periods (e.g., years or even decades) can introduce recoverability challenges, which we've discussed in the previous chapter. It is also important that image-based backups support granular recovery options. For instance, having to recover an entire virtual machine because you need to recover a single 30 KB spreadsheet within the virtual machine would be a wasteful exercise. Thankfully, most image-based backup solutions support *file-level recoverability* by 'mounting' the backup and reading from it as if it were a live system. This approach can be available for both virtual machines and block-based filesystem backups. Likewise, such backups should be readily searchable – indexing is an important function here. If you can't index a block-based backup, you may not be able to find the content you need to recover.

3.3.5 Synthetics and virtual synthetics

3.3.5.1 Overview

Backups usually offer different *levels*. While there is some variation, by and large, these levels are:

- Full: Backup all content.
- Differential: Backup all content that has changed since the last full.[7]
- Incremental: Backup all content that has changed since the last backup.

For example, a traditional weekly backup schedule would be a full backup on a Friday night, with incremental backups Saturday through to Thursday night. If a complete recovery were needed on Friday morning, you would need to recover data from the Friday full and each incremental – the backups from Saturday, Sunday, Monday, Tuesday, Wednesday, and Thursday.

Differential backups were particularly popular in tape-only backup solutions where there was a desire to run a full backup only once a month, or perhaps even less frequently. For example, consider a situation where you want to only perform a full backup once a month. If you were only doing a single full and the rest of the backups were incremental, this might result in a situation where recovery on the last day of the month resulted in reading from as many as 31 distinct backups – the full and all of the incrementals done in the month. To eliminate this possibility, differential backups might be integrated. In such a situation, you might have a schedule where you do a full backup on, say, the first Friday of the month. On all subsequent Fridays you do a differential backup. On all other days of the week, you do an incremental backup. In such a situation, the most number of backups you'd need to refer to for recovery is the full backup, the most recent differential (if one has been taken), and the incrementals generated since that most recent differential (or the full, if the recovery is within the first 7 days of the first Friday of the month).

So, where do synthetic backups fit into the picture? Synthetics stitch backups together to make a new backup. Let's consider that first example schedule – a full backup Friday night, with incremental backups on all other nights. While that reduces the amount of data that has to be read on Saturday through to Thursday, each Friday night we have to read a full copy of the data again. If the data set is large, this can be quite time-consuming. If instead a synthetic backup were taken on the next Friday, the backup process would take a new incremental backup, then 'stitch' it together with the previous full and incremental backups, creating a new (synthetic) full backup. This can still take some time to complete, but the work is done by the backup service, and the backup (as a read from the client system) completes in a relatively short time.

Virtual synthetics follow a similar approach, but offload the effort involved in creating that synthetic full backup onto the protection storage platform. If you recall Figure 3.4, you'll note that each backup image stored is a series of references to the deduplicated/compressed data blocks. This is already a 'synthetic' view of the actual backup content. A virtual synthetic operation merely extends this methodology and creates a new backup image comprising of the appropriately arranged pointers to previously captured blocks of data. When backed by an efficient architecture, virtual synthetics can be leveraged to consolidate many, large logical backups to a new logical backup image in a fraction of the time it would take to read the original data in its entirety.

3.3.5.2 How do synthetics and virtual synthetics aid recoverability?

The primary benefit that synthetics and virtual synthetics bring to recoverability is the amount of data that needs to be read from our backup clients, thereby getting us an off-platform copy sooner.

When coupled with deduplication storage, this can also result in storing more recovery points than we may have otherwise been able to. Virtual synthetics in particular can also simplify recovery selection. For instance, if you were to run every backup as a traditional full, recovery to any point in time would only require a single backup to read from. However, doing that full every day would be resource intensive and time prohibitive. However, doing a *virtual synthetic* full every day can be readily achievable, resulting in fast backup times *and* simpler recovery selection.

Virtual synthetics also make it easier, and more efficient, for deduplication storage platforms to present 'instant access' copies of data (e.g., virtual machines), which can enable additional recovery and test-recovery use cases for a business without the need for allocating additional primary storage.

3.3.6 Deletion

It may seem odd to mention deletion in the context of a discussion about improving your recoverability stance, but there are two valid reasons why you want to make sure deletion is part of your overall strategy.

Deletion in this context can refer to two different processes:

- Deleting original data (data lifecycle management) and
- Deleting backups (data protection lifecycle management)

In Greek mythology, Sisyphus was the King of Ephyra, and cheated death twice. As punishment, Hades consigned him to an eternal torment based on having to roll an extremely heavy boulder up a hill. No matter how hard he tried, the boulder would always escape him and roll back down again.

Failing to incorporate data *deletion* into your data lifecycle management process metaphorically assigns the punishment of Sisyphus to the business, and specifically IT. Without appropriate processes in place that sees data deleted when it is verifiably no longer required, the business must protect an ever-increasing amount of data. At a time when backup windows are decreasing, where businesses are asking IT to always do more with less budget, choosing to keep data that is no longer required is a Sisyphean exercise in the extreme.

In addition to deleting primary data copies when it is no longer required by the business, it's imperative that the data protection copies are deleted when they are no longer required as well. This serves two recoverability purposes: management overhead and legal liability.

For the former, since it reduces the volume of protection data under management, staff can focus on providing recoverability services for data that *needs* to be protected (and recovered).

Regarding the latter, it reduces the enforceable recovery (and potential exposure) to the legally required limits. That is, if your business is obligated for legal reasons to keep compliance backups for 7 years, you must keep those backups for 7 years. But once the 7 years have elapsed, you *should* delete those backups[8] – otherwise, in a legal discovery situation, you may be required to recover content from the backups. That they were eligible for deletion means nothing for legal discovery in many jurisdictions – if they still exist, the business can be obligated to provide them.

3.4 IMMUTABILITY

Immutability refers to ensuring data, once written, cannot be altered, or deleted. This is particularly useful in aiding recoverability since it provides both a means of meeting compliance requirements for records retention *and* helps to provide a defence layer against destructive cyber-attacks. (For that reason, we will discuss immutability in more depth in the following chapter.)

Immutability offers the following aids to recoverability within your environment:

- It can safeguard protection data against accidental or malicious modification or removal and
- It can help you ensure that you are able to meet compliance requirements (externally imposed by regulations, or internally set) for recoverability of data.

Immutability always has limits – for instance, a tape cartridge technically offers immutability because once the data has been written, you can remove the tape from its drive/library (make it offline), write-protect the tape – and the nature of how tapes are written means it is impossible to overwrite *part* of the tape without ruining the data round it. (I.e., you ostensibly cannot make undetected changes.)

But is any of that truly immutable? A write-protect tab can be overcome with ease, a tape can be loaded into another tape drive, or the cartridge itself can be opened up and the tape pulled from the spool. In essence, it is not so much truly immutable, but *procedurally immutable* with a touch of architectural immutability, rather than genuinely immutable.

In fact, all immutability in data protection will be a mix of procedural and architectural immutability. This is an important factor to keep in mind when tape adherents insist tape provides greater immutability than disk storage systems.

Disk-based immutability (standard storage systems, or object storage) has varying levels of protection. For this reason you have to be mindful when looking for immutable storage: how immutable is this? For instance, if a vendor provides documentation on how you can turn immutability off if you're running out of space and need to delete some backups, the architectural immutability is low. Other vendors providing immutability that caution you to ensure you size your solution appropriately before enabling immutability are clearly more sincere about providing a high degree of architectural immutability. For example, some vendors will caution that it is not possible for their staff (support, field services, or other) to turn immutability back off, once enabled, for stored data.

Yet are any of these storage platforms *truly* immutable? Someone with unfettered access to your datacentre and a bazooka (or even a chainsaw) would beg to differ.

So, when looking for immutability as a means of aiding recoverability, your goal is to stop thinking of *immutability* as a standalone word, and instead focus on *procedural* and *architectural* immutability. This is a shared responsibility model wherein:

1. **Procedural immutability** refers to the procedures/processes your business can put in place to defend the data physically and electronically.
2. **Architectural immutability** refers to the level of protection built into the product by the vendor to guard against deletion or alteration of data that has been flagged as immutable.

Both procedural and architectural immutability should be demonstrably *high* if you want your business to defensibly claim that it has immutable storage of data.

3.5 EXTENSIBILITY

No product exists in isolation, and data protection products are no exception. In fact, data protection products *must* interact with other systems in your environment to provide functional value. No one can provide a product so capable that without any modification it can be used to meet all your requirements. In that, we're not talking *does-it-protect-Microsoft-SQL* (though workload coverage is important), but whether you can use the product within your overall operational frameworks.

This comes down to the *extensibility* of the product. Examples of extensibility include pre- and post- scripting (ability to run custom commands or scripts, before or after backup operations, and sometimes even before or after recovery operations), adaptive licensing (see the section on Procurement later in this chapter), and comprehensive documentation. Yes, even documentation plays an important part in extensibility: if a feature is only minimally explained, how can you even begin adapting it to non-standard requirements?

Extensibility aids recoverability in a myriad of ways, some small and some significant – and all of them entirely related to *your* operational requirements. (At the bare minimum, you might say that extensibility allows the introduction of scripted, repeatable enhancements to your backup and recovery solution.)

3.6 AUTOMATION

The companion concept to extensibility is automation – the ability to have data protection systems reliably and efficiently repeat common actions. While the foundational automation requirements for data recoverability is that your data protection processes should feature automated triggering of operations based on schedules and/or observed events, automation extends significantly beyond this.

In previous IT generations, automation meant having a robust and comprehensive command line interface (CLI). While a CLI is still highly useful, more modern approaches to automation focus on deep and functional REST APIs.[9]

Automation allows you to deeply integrate data protection and recovery operations into your overall business processes. For instance, without any form of automation, someone who wants to recover data will need to have some form of domain level knowledge about that process or engage someone who does. E.g., they may need to know how to interact with a backup and recovery tool or recall data from a snapshot. If they don't know how to do this, they will need to log a service request to have someone (e.g., a backup administrator, help desk operator) to perform the recovery for them.

By comparison, automation instead allows you to build recoverability into a service portal so that a user can state what they need recovered, and the recovery can be automatically triggered. This saves the end-user from needing to know how to use the product that *does* the recovery, and saves IT time by having the recovery run without human intervention. Better still, such automation can be wrapped around business security processes and audit loggings, with the entire end-to-end process tracked and vetted for any required approvals.

Data recoverability is aided by automation in more ways than service portal integration. Developers and DBAs can use automation to repopulate dev/test systems from production backups, administrators can use it to trigger compliance check recoveries, and data scientists can use it to automatically populate data lakes and data warehouses.

3.7 SECURITY

Appropriate security is of vital importance to aiding data recoverability within an environment. If security controls are too lax, data protection systems might be abused to exfiltrate data (i.e., allow what should be an unauthorised recovery to take place) or to destroy data – we'll discuss these considerations more in the following chapter.

Likewise, if security controls are too onerous, they might *prevent* the efficient recovery of data in an emergency situation.

A CISO at a large Australian company once instituted a policy (with board agreement) that no production database could be recovered without security officer approval. This was a procedurally imposed function – i.e., technically there was nothing stopping an appropriately authorised administrator from running the recovery, but the mandated procedure was that the recovery request had to go through a security officer, and that the consequences for failing to adhere to this process would be extreme.

This procedure lasted for several months, until there was a requirement to urgently recover a critical production database out of hours. The problem? While database, platform, and data protection administrators all had a 24 × 7 on-call roster, security officers were typically not contactable out of hours. Eventually, after more than half a day of trying to get in contact with anyone from the security team, the CISO was reached for approval. Shortly thereafter, the process was 'urgently' changed to simply mandate that all recoveries had to appear in audit logs.

In an IT world where cyber-attacks are increasingly common, security has a considerable role to play in ensuring we *can* recover data when we need to. A more detailed explanation of the role security can play in recoverability is covered in Chapter 4.

3.8 PROCUREMENT

If you're wondering what procurement has to do with recoverability, the spoiler alert is: a lot. The way in which we procure data protection systems can make a significant impact to the data recoverability profile of the business. This is more than just "did you buy enough data protection storage capacity?"; it also covers features that are licensed, how licenses are measured, how licenses are renewed, and so on.

Perhaps the most overlooked part of the procurement process is: where does the budget come from? The wrong answer is *from the IT budget*. IT is *not* the home for data protection (and therefore data recoverability) budget allocation. Data protection – data recoverability – exists to service the needs of the *business* as a continuity process. As such, any mature business should allocate data protection budget from core operations budget, rather than requiring IT to pay for it. That doesn't remove the need for inspection of costs, but it does ensure the costs come from the correct bucket.

3.8.1 Licensing

3.8.1.1 Subscription, or perpetual?

As you might imagine, a perpetual licensing model grants you access to use software and the enabled features of that software in perpetuity. However, it doesn't grant perpetual access to maintenance and support for that product. For instance, you might purchase a backup and recovery product under perpetual licensing, and that purchase may include the first 3 years of software support and maintenance. After that point, in order to get any updates to the product or support for it, you would have to buy a new maintenance contract.

Subscription licensing on the other hand has a defined start and end date; once the end date has expired, the software and its functions will stop working. On the face of it, this seems undesirable; however, it can be a more predictable cost model since support and maintenance/updates are typically included in the subscription cost. So if you buy a 3-year subscription, you simply have to purchase a new subscription rather than paying for an extension of your support and maintenance for an existing product. Effectively, a lot of the decisions here come down to where your capital and operating expenditure budgets come from and how they can be consumed. (If this seems like a discussion of whether the sand comes out of a blue or a red bucket at the beach, you're probably correct – but it's no different than discussions relating to on-premises vs cloud cost models.)

Like most products, the data protection industry is moving increasingly to subscription-based licensing. (In fact, some companies have removed perpetual licensing entirely as an option.)

One key consideration for data recoverability with subscription-based licensing is the implications on transitioning between data protection products. You might use some data protection product for years – maybe even decades, and then transition your operations to a new data protection product. With perpetual licensing, you'd still be entitled to use the prior data protection product, even if you're no longer paying maintenance for it. (You would not, of course, be entitled to updates or support in such a situation. You would also likely need to maintain your own software repository, rather than expecting to be able to download those software packages in perpetuity.) Thus, if a recovery requirement were to surface *after* you'd stopped using the product, so long as it is still installed and functional, you may be able to execute the recovery. This is not the case when using subscription licensing; once the subscription expires, the software stops functioning. This means either migrating all 'legacy' compliance retention copies from the old data protection product to the new or being prepared to pay for a new subscription for the *old* product in the event of an unavoidable recovery requirement.

3.8.1.2 Measuring consumption

There are a number of different ways that licensing might be measured within data protection products. The most common variations are outlined in Table 3.1.

3.8.2 Hardware

Hardware may also require licensing, particularly in a data protection context. Dumb hardware (e.g., attaching 5×10 TB USB HDDs to a server) may require no licensing at all. However, as enhanced functionality is added to hardware platforms (storage or appliances), licensing becomes a factor. Essentially, the 'smarter' the hardware platform is in terms of introducing efficiencies into your protection environment, the more likely there will be some licensing costs associated with the hardware.

Licensing for hardware *is* often perpetual (though for *virtual appliances* this is not always the case). Again, keep in mind that the licensing is separate from the maintenance and support – you may buy a deduplication storage array with 3 years of support and maintenance built into the price, and you can continue to use it after those 3 years have elapsed, but if you want maintenance for replacing failed components or support for requesting assistance with the operating system, you'll need to pay for it.

Licensing for hardware typically covers two different areas: capacity (or platform) and features. In some situations, paying the capacity license will enable all feature functionality. In others, *some* features (e.g., immutability) may require an additional license on top of the base 'platform' cost. Sometimes, those additional features *may* be provided only under a subscription license, since they're not considered to be part of the base hardware purchase. On hardware platforms, capacity licensing may not always be reflective of the usable capacity on the system. Vendors may allow the consumer to

Table 3.1 Typical license consumption models for data protection

Consumption method	Details
Feature-based	Each distinct feature that you may wish to use within the product needs to be licensed. Backup to disk, backup to deduplicated disk, tape libraries, workload support, client counts – all of these would require separate licenses, and usually licenses are directly associated with specific elements of the configuration. (E.g., you would have to buy a tape library license for *each* tape library you attach.) This allows granular control of your licensing, but is highly inflexible – you might have 50 licenses for Oracle databases, but this doesn't help you an iota if you need to switch 10 of those databases to Microsoft SQL. Feature-based licenses typically introduce administrative overheads that don't work well in a modern, adaptive environment.
All-you-can-eat	A true all-you-can-eat license model gives you access to all features and functionality within the product to an unlimited capacity. Such licenses typically exist in only two situations: workgroup products that are not expected to be used for data intensive operations and enterprise products, where a "all things" license is required. In enterprise situations however, while all functionality at any capacity may be enabled, this will have a financial implication when calculating the yearly support and maintenance cost.
Front-end Capacity	Front-end capacity (often referred to as Front-end terabyte, or FETB) licenses allow you to protect a certain amount of data based on the size of a full copy of your environment. For instance, if you had backup software with 500 FETB licensing, any single full backup you did of your entire environment could run to 500 TB and you would be within your licensed limits. This is typically *regardless* of how many copies you generate, or how long you keep those copies for. In most instances (though not guaranteed), this enables all functionality within the product – effectively, an 'all you can eat' model but with a guardrail that allows the restaurant to eject you if you try to eat too much.
Back-end Capacity	Back-end capacity (often referred to as Back-end terabyte, or BETB) licenses allow you to protect as much data as you want to, so long as your backup storage utilisation does not exceed the licensed amount. For instance, if you have 500 BETB licensing, it doesn't matter how large or small your environment is that you want to protect, or how many copies of data you want to keep, or how long you want to keep those copies for – but they must all fit within 500 TB. BETB is often used in service provider models, especially where service providers are using deduplication storage. It can also be used for data protection *appliances* that integrate a hardware and software solution.

(Continued)

Table 3.1 (Continued) Typical license consumption models for data protection

Consumption method	Details
Unit	Unit-based licensing is often another variation of the all-you-can-eat model, but rather than limiting based on FETB or BETB, you limit based on other measurable consumption units. This might be the number of virtual machines in your environment, the number of databases you're protecting, or the number of cores (or sockets – and there can be a large difference) being used to run your environment. Some vendors may even use formulas that allow a single 'logical' unit to be consumed regardless of whether it's for a virtual machine, database, or appliance. E.g., a base unit might be calculated as being the equivalent of a 2 GHz CPU core. A database of up to 1 TB might require a single unit, between 1 and 10 may require 5 units, and so on. Unit-based licensing is often favoured in heterogeneous environments.

buy a particular block of physical storage (e.g., one shelf of disks), but attach to it a license for just half of the usable storage this presents. This can allow businesses to increase capacity more granularly (which is an important consideration as hard drive sizes continue to increase).

Even hardware licensing can aid recoverability. After all, implementation and ongoing development of advanced functionality (e.g., deduplication and immutability) can consume much engineering effort within a vendor, and the licensing of hardware platforms ensures that this functionality continues to be worked on.

3.8.3 In-cloud

You may have compliance retention requirements for your data. Your obligations do not pass to your cloud service provider. This is critically important when it comes to data recoverability within the cloud. While there may be grace periods involved, once you stop paying a subscription to cloud services, the cloud service provider can (and will) delete your data.

In Section 2.8.3, examples of ongoing operating costs for cloud storage services were provided as an example of how your data protection costs may grow when using the public cloud. What is important to keep in mind though is that there can be a significant difference to what happens to data you need to recover from when you stop paying a vendor depending on whether you're on-premises or in the public-cloud. In an on-premises situation, if you've purchased the storage array the data resides on, even if you stop paying the support and maintenance to the vendor, you at least retain physical ownership of the data; you can still (at a fundamental level at least) claim that you are meeting recovery compliance requirements. In the public cloud, however, at some point after you stop paying for the data storage, the cloud provider will stop storing the data.

That's not meant to be some campfire-scary story intended to keep your protection data on-premises – the point more is that once you make the commitment to put data in the public cloud that you may wish to recover from at a later point, you need to be prepared to *continue* to pay for it for the recovery lifespan, or have contingency plans in place if you want to *stop* paying for it.

3.9 PROCESSES AND DOCUMENTATION

The most efficient and powerful technology in the world offers little benefit if you are unable to properly use it. This applies to data protection as much as any other technology. While many IT personnel find documentation frustrating to write, and procedures at times stifling to follow, these both play a critical role in enabling recoverability within a business.

Documentation can aid in three different ways. First, documentation can outline exactly how a data protection system should be configured (globally, and at a granular level – e.g., "how to add a FreeBSD system to the backup environment") in a way that folds it into the data protection processes.

Additionally, documentation can be critical in addition to providing instructions on *how* data recovery can be facilitated. Since recovery is a business function, documentation is more than purely technical instructions – it can capture a potential myriad of organisational elements of a recovery, including (but not limited to) approval processes, notification methods, emergency budget options, and security considerations. Continuity documentation will even cover processes around power, telephony, and building access, with the technical recovery documentation being just one aspect. Finally, documentation can also capture the key rebuild-state information that needs to be referenced if that recovery must start from a first principles approach: e.g., reinstall operating systems, applications, or appliances from a console, inputting essential configuration details by hand.

Processes (particularly when coupled with documentation) can play a critical recoverability aid, including but not limited to the following scenarios:

- Allowing new staff to come up to speed quickly during a recovery situation
- Allowing existing staff who may be cognitively compromised (e.g., a sleepy administrator who has been woken at 2 am) or highly stressed (e.g., during a disaster recovery situation) to refer to a known good sequence of steps to complete a recovery
- Allowing staff who are not domain experts to complete a recovery by following clear steps (e.g., help desk staff recovering an operating system)
- Allowing the business to prove to auditors that data recovery processes are structured and repeatable

The success of data recovery situations is highly dependent on whether the process can be completed in the correct order, without endangering any other data in the environment. Adequate documentation and processes is an essential aspect of eliminating human error from these situations.

 LESSON TEN: No technology can save your business from an untrained user with privileged access who doesn't know how to use the environment you've placed them in.

3.10 WRAPPING UP

There are a multitude of different technologies and options that can be used in a data protection environment, and each of them can either aid (or hinder) recoverability depending on how they are used and how your environment has been architected and implemented. It's critical therefore to ensure you pick the right options and technology and use them in such a way that they maximise your ability to recover data if – or when – it is required.

NOTES

1 https://meroli.web.cern.ch/blog_cern_questions.html
2 https://techuda.com/largest-hard-drive-in-the-world-western-digital-26tb-hdd/
3 https://www.techradar.com/best/large-hard-drives-and-ssds
4 It was not uncommon in the early days of snapshot solutions to see businesses attempt to save costs by using cheaper (and slower) hard drives for snapshot storage. E.g., snapshot storage space allocated from 5400 RPM drives while the data being protected resided on 10K or 15K RPM drives. As change rates built up on snapshots, the overall system performance would be pulled down to match the 5400 RPM drives that were trying to keep up with writes.
5 https://aws.amazon.com/s3/faqs/
6 For public cloud storage, compression isn't so much about increasing the number of copies we can store, but decreasing the cost of the copies we store.
7 This assumes a 'flat' differential method. Some products may support multi-level differentials, where a differential can either refer back to a full, or a lower/same numbered differential, but an overview of the mechanics of this approach is not necessary to understand synthetic fulls.
8 Of course, legal obligations may vary. For instance, if a court case is underway, the data may need to be kept longer. Some jurisdictions also impose a statute of limitations on data retention after a court case has been completed that can run into years.
9 Representational State Transfer (REST) Application Programming Interface (API) refers to a means of engaging with product functionality through effectively stateless web-based operations ('put', 'get', 'delete', etc.).

Chapter 4

Building recovery into cyber resilience

4.1 INTRODUCTION

Like other industries, IT has some truisms in it. "RAID is not backup" is one that springs to mind in a data protection context. The central theme to this chapter revolves around another truism:

There are only two types of businesses: those who have been hit by ransomware, and those who haven't been hit yet

This reflects a changing focus in information security approaches. Earlier, naive approaches to information security practices focused on establishing bigger walls around the business – i.e., perimeter defence using firewalls, demilitarised zones, etc. (Interior defence was often centred around virus scanning.) Much like a cheesy horror movie ("the call is coming from inside the house!"), more modern and sophisticated approaches to information security work on a clear assumption that threats are already present on the internal network.

Being able to recover data won't save you from every form of cyber-attack. We can classify the usefulness of recovery in a cyber-attack as either a *primary* solution or a support tool for analysis. If someone breaks into your systems and deletes the contents of your primary storage array, recovery will be a primary solution. If on the other hand, you've been hit by a data breach, recoveries may help you with forensic examination (e.g., retrieving logs that were deleted to hide the attack), but the primary concern is about data exfiltration, not data loss.

DOI: 10.1201/9781032624952-4

Having a secure recoverability solution is a paramount defence against destructive cyber-attacks. For some businesses, being unable to recover has meant a permanent closure:

An American healthcare provider, Wood Ranch Medical, also had to shut down its services due to a cyber attack in 2019. The facility suffered a ransomware attack in August 2019, locking them out of the patients' data.

According to reports, the attack caused irreparable damage to the infected systems making file recovery impossible.

Eventually Wood Ranch Medical announced a permanent closure of services until December 17, 2019.

"6 times when hackers forced companies to go bankrupt and shut down", Abeerah Hashim, 14 September 2022, PrivacySavvy. https:// privacysavvy.com/security/business/6-times-hackers-forced-companies-to-go-bankrupt-shut-down/

In this chapter we'll focus on the situations where recovery can serve as a primary solution.

LESSON ELEVEN: A cyber resiliency plan that doesn't include recovery is not a plan at all.

4.2 RECOVERY'S PLACE IN THE NIST FRAMEWORK

The National Institute of Standards and Technology (NIST) Cybersecurity Framework[1] serves as an excellent reference point for why you'd integrate recovery into your cyber resilience strategy. The core of the framework cites the following five framework functions:

- Identify
- Protect
- Detect
- Respond
- Recover

In short: a comprehensive cyber resilience strategy will accept the risk that data *can* be lost or destroyed and will require recovery. Not every attack can be detected and repulsed in time to avoid a data loss situation.

Recover – Develop and implement appropriate activities to maintain plans for resilience and to restore any capabilities or services that were impaired due to a cybersecurity incident.

The Recover Function supports timely recovery to normal operations to reduce the impact from a cybersecurity incident. Examples of outcome Categories within this Function include: Recovery Planning; Improvements; and Communications.

NIST Cybersecurity Framework v1.1, April 16, 2018, https://nvl pubs.nist.gov/nistpubs/CSWP/NIST.CSWP.04162018.pdf

---

We will leave the security aspects of the Cybersecurity Framework aside; these constitute a wholly separate domain with their own areas of expertise – instead, in this chapter, we'll focus on the recovery aspect of cyber resilience.

4.3 THREAT VECTORS REQUIRING CYBER RESILIENCE

It's easy to think that cyber resilience comes down to having a method of recovering from a ransomware attack. However, there are several vectors that drive a need to consider building recovery into a cyber resilience strategy.

4.3.1 Ransomware and deletionware

Functionally, both ransomware and deletionware fulfil the same purpose – they destroy your data. The former, by encrypting it and demanding a ransom for the decryption key, the latter, by simply erasing it. In either case, your data has been destroyed. Some would argue that the data attacked by ransomware isn't destroyed, but paying a ransom is not a desirable strategy: you're (a) assuming that the attacker is honourable enough to have a decryption key available and (b) establishing that *your business is a good target*.

These two types of viruses are typically introduced into the business network through either malicious or accidental actors and are becoming increasingly sophisticated as the cyber-attack market grows in revenue.

While primitive forms of these viruses will attack whatever system they are introduced on to, more advanced forms also include worm-like functionality, where they will seek to spread on the network, finding known vulnerabilities, administrator credentials, and even backup systems.

The pentesters [Conti ransomware team members] search specifically for Veeam privileged users and services and which they can then leverage to access, exfiltrate, remove and encrypt backups to ensure their ransomware demands are not hindered by this last line of defense [sic].

"Veeam backups targeted by the Conti ransomware group", David, May 26 2022, Blocky for Veeam, https://blockyforveeam.us/veeam-backups-targeted-by-the-conti-ransomware-group

---

After all, if a virus can destroy your backups, you may be *forced* to pay a ransom to get your data back. This is where a cyber resilience solution built with recovery in mind can be helpful.

4.3.2 Careless and socially engineered employees

Not all insider attacks are malicious. Mistakes happen; that may be because employees are insufficiently trained, or temporarily impaired (e.g., they have a newborn baby, have insomnia, or were groggy on a 2 am support call), careless, made a typo, or any number of other situations.

A senior Unix systems administrator once configured an automount mesh on all systems, such that every server's filesystem was accessible under /a/servername. Not long after that was configured, he was doing some clean-up on a server and as root, ran a command along the lines of "rm -rf /$TMPDIR". Unfortunately, the variable he used wasn't defined, so the system faithfully ran "rm -rf /"; after the command had been running a while, he stopped it and realised it had been enumerating through the server filesystems mounted under /a.

While a careless employee may not *technically* qualify as a cyber-attack, the havoc they can wreak on systems within your environment (particularly when they have elevated privilege levels) can be significant – and call for similar recovery techniques as those required during cyber-attacks.

Another area where employees may be compromised is via social engineering. An employee might be convinced – either by the perceived urgency or validity of a request – to access a website, provide their credentials, or download a binary that can be used to introduce malware or a malicious actor onto the network. (Such is the risk of social engineering that many businesses focus much, if not all, of their end-user security education on *phishing tests*, sending out fake emails to see which users will click on them and requiring those who fail the test to attend training.)

4.3.3 Malicious employees

There are several reasons that an employee may become malicious. This can include situations such as:

- Insufficient (or believed insufficient) remuneration
- External factors (debt, stress, extortion, etc.)
- Resentment (work hours, duties, lack of advancement, etc.)
- Genuine ill-intent
- Desire for notoriety
- Business taken over by a billionaire who sacks more than half the staff and demands the remaining staff work 80+ hours a week
- Intent to prove internal issues

Regardless of the driving factors, malicious employees represent a higher risk than careless employees simply because the attacks they engage in are not accidental – they're deliberate, regardless of whether they are spur-of-the-moment or well planned.

While malicious employees are more often considered risks for data breaches (and they certainly represent a risk on that front), they can also place the business at risk of data destruction. The risk posed by malicious employees is significant – particularly those with elevated privileges – because they *know* where sensitive data and systems can be found and may even have direct access to them. They may also be aware of internal vulnerabilities that can be exploited for increased access and/or hide their tracks, such as insecure access points, hardcoded passwords, or unpatched breaches.

Malicious employees can also include ex-employees who still have access:

> After being terminated, however, JOHNSON remotely accessed the plant's computer system and intentionally transmitted code and commands which resulted in significant damage to Georgia-Pacific and its operations.
>
> "Former Systems Administrator Sentenced to Prison for Hacking into Industrial Facility Computer System", United States Justice Department, February 16 2017.[2]

Indeed, it is this sort of attack (from a recently dismissed employee) that leads businesses to integrate user account management with Human Resources (HR) databases – so that systems access is automatically cancelled as soon as a HR system records the employee as terminated. Though, it must be noted, this only works when there are no "generic" access accounts that can be logged into (e.g., "root", or "Administrator" accounts).

4.3.4 Hacktivism

Hacktivism is a portmanteau of "hacking" and "activism" and refers to a growing challenge posed by people who take activism into the electronic frontiers. A Norton blog on Hacktivism defines it as "the misuse of a computer or the internet to expose a believed injustice."[3]

Whereas in the past activists agitating for a cause might have focused on physical damage and disruption – dumping manure in front of corporate headquarters, invading shareholder meetings, and so on – new avenues might include disruption of web services, leaking of sensitive information, and damage to corporate systems.

Like other forms of cyber-attacks, it's likely this problem will continue to rise – and a frank assessment of the state of the world perhaps explains why: climate change, excessive corporate profits while workers must choose between feeding their family or heating their homes, and a massive disparity between the haves and the have-nots affecting housing, health, and general well-being can only serve to accentuate the desire of some to raise awareness to problems however they can.

It's common to assume that hacktivists may have good intentions, even if their actions have dubious ethical justification. Anonymous and Wikileaks for instance both claim to act for transparency and social/political justice, and when hacktivists supporting Ukraine took over Russian streaming services to broadcast details of atrocities committed by the invading army,[4] it seems easy enough to cheer them on. Yet not all hacktivism is so easily defended; hacktivism is just as likely to come from people supporting immoral causes (attacking renewable energy to encourage fossil fuel usage, spreading misinformation about climate change, supporting dictatorial regimes, etc.), and the toolkits and methods used by hacktivists for both good and evil are usually the same.

4.3.5 Industrial attack

Not all businesses and actors within the business space operate ethically. Industrial attacks (e.g., corporate espionage) are often associated with the theft of trade secrets, but in an era where most trade secrets are kept electronically, causing damage to systems to hide an attack is the modern-day equivalent to setting fire to a warehouse to hide a break-in.

Increasingly, industrial attacks seem to be state-sponsored, or at least state-allowed:

"An Israeli-American cybersecurity firm said Monday that it uncovered a "massive" hacking operation, apparently led by a hacking group believed to be backed by China, that had engaged in intellectual property (IP) theft and industrial espionage on three continents."

"US-Israeli cyber firm uncovers 'massive' Chinese-backed industrial espionage ring", Ricky Ben-David, 9 May 2022, The Times of Israel, https://www.timesofisrael.com/us-israeli-cyber-firm-uncovers-massive-chinese-backed-industrial-espionage-ring/

While it is indisputable that most industrial attacks are focused on data exfiltration rather than data destruction, the risk to a business when an attacker is residing within its systems (sometimes for many months) remains substantial.

4.3.6 Nation-state attack

Sometimes an attacker is not an individual, hacktivist, or competitor, but a nation-state actor. One of the most frequently held up examples of this is Sony and North Korea[5]; this is referenced so frequently not because there are so *few* cases, but because it remains one of the most publicly known examples of where a nation-state has almost destroyed a business.

Yet, the Sony/North Korea incident was not the first such incident, nor was it the last. Electronic digital warfare was used with considerable success against Iran with the Stuxnet attack in 2010.[6] While they strenuously denied it, China was named as the likely attacker against the Australian Bureau of Meteorology in 2015.[7] In September 2022:

> "Albania severed diplomatic relations with Iran on Wednesday and kicked out its diplomats after a cyberattack in July it blamed on the Islamic Republic, a move Washington supported as it vowed to take action in response to the attack on its NATO ally."
>
> Reuters, September 8 2022, https://www.reuters.com/world/albania-cuts-iran-ties-orders-diplomats-go-after-cyber-attack-pm-says-2022-09-07/

Governments around the world are encouraging increased vigilance against cyber-attacks for businesses in a variety of sensitive industry verticals including transport, logistics, healthcare, energy infrastructure, defence, public services, other utilities, and of course financial sectors. Given the scope for disruption to an entire country following a successful cyber-attack against one of these industries, it is no wonder that they attract attention from so many types of attackers.

Industries that have a mix of Information Technology and Operational Technology (OT) networks are perhaps particularly at risk in nation-state attack situations. Businesses running OT networks, such as energy networks, manufacturing, and primary industries, have traditionally focused security concerns on their IT networks, leaving OT network administrators to deliver *security-by-obfuscation* and air-gapped security models. Security by obfuscation is a dead-end approach in the face of rapacious attackers, and hard gaps between IT and OT are frequently blurred for the sake of convenience, or in the desire to reach cloud services. As a result, OT networks with poor security oversight are now more readily accessible to attackers:

In an analysis published on Tuesday, Microsoft researchers said they had discovered a vulnerable open-source component in the Boa web server, which is still widely used in a range of routers and security cameras, as well as popular software development kits (SDKs), despite the software's retirement in 2005. The technology giant identified the component while investigating a suspected Indian electric grid intrusion first detailed by Recorded Future in April, where Chinese state-sponsored attackers used IoT devices to gain a foothold on operational technology (OT) networks, used to monitor and control physical industrial systems.

Microsoft said it has identified one million internet-exposed Boa server components globally over the span of a one-week period, warning that the vulnerable component poses a "supply chain risk that may affect millions of organizations and devices."

"Microsoft says attackers are hacking energy grids by exploiting decades-old software" Carly Page, 24 November 2022, Yahoo! News, https://au.news.yahoo.com/microsoft-says-attackers-hacking-energy-141830647.html

---

Regardless of whether attacks come from nation-state attackers or closer to home, the state of security (or a lack thereof) within OT networks will play an increasing role in the cyber-attack landscape over the coming years.

4.4 CONSIDERATIONS FOR RECOVERABILITY IN CYBER RESILIENCE

Now we've considered the primary threat vectors for cyber-attacks, we can consider some basic strategies that should be implemented to build recoverability into a cyber resilience plan.

Building recoverability into your cyber resilience posture is a three-stage process; depending on the sensitivity of your business or

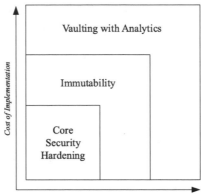

Figure 4.1 The three stages to integrate recoverability into cyber resilience.

available budget, you may choose not to implement all three stages, but you should carefully evaluate your needs and budgetary options.

The three stages, as outlined in Figure 4.1, offer progressively better protection, but each layer of protection adds another layer of cost. They are:

1. Core security hardening
2. Immutability
3. Vaulting with Analytics

We'll discuss each of these in the following sections.

4.4.1 Core security hardening

At a bare minimum, it's essential to build strict security practices into your data protection systems. This encompasses activities including but not limited to:

- Adequate password protection
- Role-based access controls
- Limited access to administrative accounts
- Comprehensive audit logging
- Multifactor authentication whenever it is supported
- Applying patches in a timely fashion after they're released
- Minimising 'desktop' access to a backup server, and
- Disabling insecure access protocols

Most backup vendors will produce security hardening guides, and these should be followed carefully to reduce the threat surface presented by the data protection product to the rest of your network.

It is an irony that many businesses have a lackadaisical attitude towards access security *within* backup and recovery environments. The purpose of a backup and recovery solution within your environment is to allow you to protect your most important datasets. Many businesses, for sure, backup everything in their environments. But more accurately, almost *all* businesses have some form of backup and recovery service protecting their mission-critical and other production workloads/data sets – even if non-production systems (e.g., test and development staging systems) are not backed up.

So, let's walk back from talking about backup and recovery as a *function* and dwell on the *implications* of backup and recovery within a security context.

Your backup and recovery systems can retrieve data from practically anywhere within your network. Your backup and recovery systems can write data to practically anywhere within your network.

There are several layers of risk that backup and recovery systems introduce into an environment that should encourage you to always approach them as requiring the highest security standards:

1. Destruction of backups
2. Missing backups or reducing protection
3. Corrupting live data

In a ransomware context, the first item is perhaps understood most readily within modern corporate environments: if effectively designed ransomware (or similar attacks) gain access to your backup environment, it may be possible to encrypt, delete, or otherwise compromise the data held in your backups. Even if immutability has been achieved for the backup storage itself, the backup service is still potentially at risk of its catalogue and configuration information being destroyed, resulting in a costly interruption to operations.

Missing backups, or reducing protection, could be achieved via introducing undetected changes to the backup systems configuration. For instance, an attacker might turn off backup policies, so they don't run, remove replication steps from policies, thereby preventing the creation of offsite copies, or perhaps more insidiously adjust either the start time of policies (e.g., reducing a runtime window from 20:00 to 08:00 to 23:59 to 00:01) or the frequency at which they're run (from daily, to weekly).

The third scenario effectively involves misusing the fundamental intention of a backup service, turning it into a data destruction system. Consider, for instance, a compromised backup system that:

- Recovers corrupt /etc/passwd and /etc/shadow files to every Linux or Unix host in an environment
- Performs relocated recoveries until systems fill up and become unusable
- Recovers 2-week-old copies of databases over existing production databases
- Randomly, intermittently recovers old copies of files on a NAS – few enough files any day to be noticed, but difficult to fix once finally detected

While there are a variety of enterprise backup products, there is not infinite variety. We have already seen examples of ransomware attacks which seek out backup servers to destroy backups as a means of encouraging payment; at some point hackers and criminal gangs will undoubtedly start using compromised backup and recovery systems to achieve their goals.

Returning to the original premise: many organisations have lackadaisical approaches to security for their backup and recovery systems. The opposite must be true for even a foundational approach to cyber resilience: your backup and recovery systems must leverage *at least* the same level of access and operational security (if not more than) as your *most critical data sets*.

Businesses with mature security teams are increasingly focused on real-time access to data protection audit logs so these sorts of attacks can be detected or at least traced once discovered. While human users of a system may not immediately notice configuration changes, for instance, an automated analysis system that receives audit log details of all configuration changes may detect such changes and raise alerts if they are unaccompanied by approval tags (e.g., service request IDs).

4.4.2 Immutability, Redux

A bare minimum step towards ensuring recoverability is part of your cyber resilience strategy is to work with immutable backups. If a backup cannot be erased or corrupted, you have a higher chance of being able to retrieve it in the event of the original data being attacked.

On initial analysis, does this call for tape? Tape backups, after all, can be (a) removed from a system and (b) stored in a physically isolated environment. Yet, despite those benefits, tape introduces some impracticalities. For example:

- Your recovery speed is limited to the number of tape drives you can simultaneously stream from
- Recoveries can only be executed in parallel against any individual tape if the backups were executed in parallel – i.e., tapes do not support concurrent, randomised access of multiple backups
- Writable tapes which are in a tape library or drive may be compromised if the backup server is attacked
- If you're planning sophisticated scanning of your backups for signs of cyber-attacks, tape is usually not compatible

In general, tape should be seen only as an immutable option for businesses that are unable to allocate sufficient budget for robust, practical cyber recovery operations. Remember that few businesses would rely on tape only to recover their datacentres in the event of a significant disaster, and while disaster recoveries and cyber recoveries may have different SLAs, the applicability of tape for mass recoveries remains the same in both situations.

It is increasingly common for data protection storage appliances (e.g., deduplication storage for backups) to offer immutable storage. This might be referred to as immutable, Write Once Read Many (WORM) or retention lock, but the goal remains the same no matter the nomenclature used.

Immutable in this sense *must* mean truly immutable, not *immutable until you desire otherwise*. For example, a combination of high architectural immutability and high procedural immutability. An 'immutable' solution that includes knowledge-base articles on how to temporarily turn off immutability if you're running out of

storage capacity is not a truly immutable solution. To be functionally effective in the face of increasingly sophisticated cyber-attacks,
immutability needs to be comprehensibly applied – not just in day-
to-day operations, but in all extraordinary circumstances. Of course,
this is not *just* to defend against cyber-attacks – it's also an essential
aspect of regulatory compliance. Referring to the Sarbanes-Oxley
Act of 2002:

Section 802 makes it a crime to knowingly alter, destroy, mutilate, con-
ceal, cover-up, falsify, or make a false entry in any record, document,
or tangible object with the intent to "impede, obstruct or influence"
any federal investigation of any matter or any title 11 bankruptcy case.
This includes those acts committed in relation to or contemplation of
any such matter or case.

   Whoever commits such crime is subject to a fine, imprisonment of
not more than 20 years, or both.

"Sarbanes-Oxley Act of 2002", Akiko Yamada, May 21 2021, Law Blog
101. https://lawblog101.com/sarbanes-oxley-act-of-2002-section-802/

For example, having a "immutable unless we want otherwise" data
protection storage platform has the potential to expose your business to significant legal risk in addition to any additional risks relating to malware and other attacks that encrypt or delete your data.

4.5 VAULTING

It's no coincidence that both banking and cyber resilience use the
term *vaulting*. Advanced cyber recovery capabilities have been
driven by programs such as *Sheltered Harbor*.

Sheltered Harbor's purpose is to protect customers, financial institu-
tions, and public confidence in the financial system if a catastrophic
event like a cyber attack causes an institution's critical systems –
including backups – to fail.

About page, Sheltered Harbor, https://shelteredharbor.org/about

---

Sheltered Harbor describes themselves as:

> A not-for-profit subsidiary of FS-ISAC (Financial Services Information Sharing and Analysis Center), the Sheltered Harbor organization is devoted to coordinating the development of the Sheltered Harbor standard, promoting adoption across the industry, supporting implementation, and ensuring adherence.
>
> Ibid.

Sheltered Harbor consists of a *data vault* and a *resiliency plan*. Once participating financial organisations have these in place, they can apply for certification and attest their readiness for dealing with a cyber-attack. The organisation defines the data vault as follows:

> Institutions back up critical customer account data each night in the Sheltered Harbor standard format, either managing their own vault or using a participating service provider. The data vault is encrypted, unchangeable, and completely separated from the institution's infrastructure, including all backups.
>
> How it Works, Sheltered Harbor, https://shelteredharbor.org/how-it-works

While the focus of Sheltered Harbor is organisations operating within the financial institution sphere in the United States, the operational principles outlined – i.e., data vaulting for secure recovery in the event of a destructive attack on the IT infrastructure of a business – can be readily adapted and applied to almost all organisations, regardless of their size, country, or industry vertical.

Electronic vaulting then works on the same principle as vaulting within banks; by locking away valuable content in a vault, the goal is to preserve that content even if someone with nefarious plans enters the building where normal operations take place. A minimum scope vault configuration is shown in Figure 4.2.

A vault will exist separate to any production/primary or failover/disaster recovery datacentres, though the nature of the separation may vary. There will be an air gap between the vault and one of the

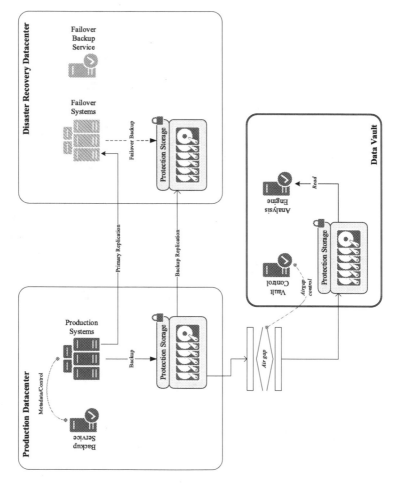

Figure 4.2 Basic vault configuration.

protection storage platforms in the regular datacentres. This air gap will be active by default (i.e., no traffic can pass through). Control systems operating *within* the vault will periodically deactivate the air gap, allowing data replication traffic to take place. No other incoming traffic is permitted from the regular datacentres and the vault. (This would typically be enforced with a firewall operating within the vault – irrespective of any firewall that may be active in the source datacentre.)

Once data has been ingested into the vault, it will ideally be scanned for signs of compromise – we will discuss the scanning later.

In most circumstances, there will be additional systems within the vault (or even a *clean room*) so that data can be safely recovered within the secure, isolated environment in the event of a production systems compromise. For the remainder of this chapter, we'll discuss key aspects of vault operations.

4.5.1 Separation

4.5.1.1 Operational

Vaults are established to provide recovery against even the most extreme of cyber-attacks, and these attacks are at their most crippling when insiders are involved – either deliberately or accidentally.

It is important then for vaults to run via *operational* separation. This means that under no circumstance should staff who have access to standard production networks and systems have access to the vault – and vice versa.

This operational separation can be achieved through having different teams within the business manage the vault. For example, while the infrastructure team manages the production backup and recovery services, the security team may manage the vault. However, this can create challenges: security in itself is a whole domain of knowledge and requiring security professionals to develop backup and recovery skillsets may meet with friction.

Particularly for larger businesses, running a vault via managed services or outsourcing can be an efficient approach. A service provider may run vaults for many businesses and develop deep technical skills while not having any access to the production data protection operations of their clients. Running a vault is not a full-time operation, and so should be considerably cheaper than a full-time managed service contract (though there will need to be a capability to quickly scale up vault staffing in the event of needing to onboard new workloads, conduct tests, or conduct bulk recoveries in the event of an attack).

4.5.1.2 Physical

A bank vault may be located within bank, but it will be physically separated by plate walls and its own door. Likewise, vaults used for cyber resilience will also require physical separation. Vaults might be housed in a separate datacentre from the primary networks, or they might be in the same datacentre, but be physically locked away and require different access protocols.

While electronic separation (see following) is vitally important for a vault, it is useless without physical separation, since a malicious attacker could use physical access to the vault to either physically destroy equipment or introduce electronic attacks into the vault, bypassing any air gap or firewalled access.

Physical separation, therefore, is more than just having the vault in a different location, or requiring different permissions to enter. It is also about what items can be carried *into* the vault. For instance, USB-keys (or drives), laptops, even cellular phones, and tablets should be prohibited. Such items are either permanently within the vault or never in the vault – there should be no ingress of anything that might be used to inflict damage. Likewise, this should include removal of anything that might be used to breach the air gap wirelessly – e.g., laptops that reside in the vault should have WiFi interfaces *removed*, not just disabled. Such a strategy should apply to any cellular/radio connectivity, too. (Modern datacentres already often have strict controls over what may be taken inside, so this should be a natural extension of that policy.)

This approach requires careful planning on two fronts:

- How to restore data from the vault and
- How to update vault systems

For the former, the last thing you want to do when trying to restore from the vault is to move system(s) into the vault to recover onto, only to have those systems enter infected, and cause challenges within the vault. This means either having a safe data egress path planned out for vault recoveries or having known clean, blank systems available in or near to the vault to recover on to. We will cover this in more detail in a later section ("Clean rooms").

Regarding the latter, a key element of successful vault security is minimising the amount of *executable data* in the vault. For example, a vault remains relatively secure by the very nature of its configuration so long as data that is copied into the vault is only *read* and not *executed* against. This works up to the point where you need to actually update the software and services running in the vault. How can you therefore reliably get this content into the vault without risking the systems running in there? The answer is in the vaulting process itself – any updates to vault software should be transferred via the standard, secure vaulting process and verified by the vault processing systems as being safe, before being used to update vault systems. This will provide a greater degree of security than simply carrying in a USB key.

4.5.1.3 Electronic

Finally, electronic separation is required for successful vault operations. This is across all potential incoming vectors. For example, while an air gap is used to control when connectivity is permitted for incoming replication, that should be the only traffic allowed into the vault. This means the vault should be entirely self-sufficient for basic services such as hostname resolution, time synchronisation and account authentication – there should be no reliance on any production service. (Time synchronisation within a vault is often accomplished via a dedicated cellular system.)

Electronic separation also helps to achieve operational separation; if entirely independent user authentication systems are used in primary systems compared to vault systems, there is less chance of having accounts that have access to both environments.

Electronic separation does not necessarily have to be bidirectional. It is typically useful to allow reporting and alerting initiated within the vault to propagate outside of the vault for real-time visibility. Thus, a minimal number of outgoing ports may be permitted – e.g., it may be possible to send basic email from within the vault to an external system. Control processes can be put in place to ensure this is not abused. Critically, any control system utilised should be housed and active *within* the vault, thereby denying the opportunity for external control. Two standard options are:

- **Firewalls** – a more traditional network control approach whereby any traffic that attempts to come *in* the link present for email is blocked by a system within the vault.

- **Data diodes** – a data diode offers a higher level of surety over a firewall by physically only supporting monodirectional traffic. A data diode may be placed on a network link between the vault and external systems to allow outgoing email; in such a configuration, while email traffic can *exit* the vault over the data diode, it is *physically impossible* for any traffic to pass over the data diode from the external network back into the vault.

Obviously, there is a functional dichotomy relating to a vault. It needs to be air-gapped to provide maximum protection from intrusion. But there is also a need to periodically allow replication from a production source to the vault so that the vault has useful, recoverable data in it.

Another approach to air-gapping is limited physical connectivity; for instance, instead of achieving incoming replication via switches and firewalls, it may be preferable to instead have an ethernet or optical cable directly connected between a production data protection storage system and the vault storage system. Interfaces on the vault storage system can still be enabled or disabled to create the air gap, but when the air gap isn't active, there is only one system that can transmit communicate into the vault.

4.5.2 What should you vault?

In an ideal world, we'd vault everything. After all, if you run backup services against it, it must be important data, right?

Vaulting adds a layer of cost to your operations, however. Does non-critical data (e.g., development and test systems, lower-tier file-storage, and so on) require the same level of protection of the most critical data the business handles? For most businesses, the answer is a firm no. This means taking an onion-skin approach to your protection.

Recall in Figure 4.1, the view for building recoverability into your cyber resiliency strategy was to consider three different levels:

1. Security hardening
2. Immutability
3. Vaulting with analytics

While security hardening should be conducted regardless of the situation, immutable backups may provide adequate defence for non-critical systems. Vaulting can therefore be reserved for the most crucial data and platforms within the business. You can often approach the question of "what to vault" by asking the question, "what data/platforms are so critical that if they cease to exist, our business also ceases to exist?" This isn't to say that the business immediately vanishes if the data does (although such data would obviously fit the bill); it also refers to the data that is essential for day-to-day operations – where, in the event of it being lost, the clock will be ticking on the health of the business.

There are typically three different types of data and platforms that will be considered under this banner of criticality. These are:

1. Essential IT functions
2. Essential operational data
3. Mission-critical business functions

Mission-critical business functions are ironically the easiest to understand, but often the most difficult to identify within an organisation. For a logistics company for instance, this might start by focusing on everything to do with shipping – tracking incoming parcels, parcels moving throughout the business network, and then the delivery platforms. But, when businesses often have hundreds or thousands of applications and services, there will be many inter-dependencies, and many groups will consider their systems to be "mission-critical". Thus, the systems and data that support these business functions need to be carefully evaluated by all business units, with the IT department providing insight.

Essential IT functions are what can be described as the backbone services for the company. These include low-level information such as domain name services (DNS), active directory (AD), and network switch configuration dumps. Other details might include custom certificates and even essential software licenses.

Essential operational data, in short, relates to business banking and employee services. To be sure, "we can't pay you until we can fix this problem" might be an excellent motivator for staff to work around the clock to resolve business issues, but *why should they?* No one could blame staff for feeling insecure and looking for a new job if their current employer needs to completely rebuild payroll information and re-gain access to its banking systems before they can be paid. Even more simply, if the business has lost core systems such as AD, how will staff be *contacted* to help coordinate a cyber recovery? Storing copies of emergency contact lists and personal staff email addresses/phone numbers could literally mean a difference of *days* to a recovery situation if normal communication services (email, instant messaging, etc.) are down.

Particularly when it comes to essential operational data and essential IT function data, special attention should be paid to data formats and special recovery scenarios. Consider, for instance, the example of being able to contact staff in the event of AD services being destroyed. This might create a *chicken-and-the-egg* scenario: (a) you need to recover active directory, but (b) this requires contacting staff who *can* do the recovery. However, (c) you can't contact the staff because their primary contact details were in active directory, and (d) the HR database that also stores staff contact details requires active directory to be present for a recovery to succeed.

Whenever you consider cyber event recoveries, you need to assume that all your essential systems are gone. This means some of the absolute 'basic' data, such as network switch configs, DNS details, and yes, staff contact lists, should be backed up not only in their native format, but in *human consumable format*, too. To bootstrap the company, you may need to recover basic text files that have no dependencies so you can manually build up enough configuration to run a better, faster, and more automated recovery process. In this, approaching the vault like an actual physical vault makes sense: if you had to *print out* core bootstrap information for storage in an on-site vault, how could you make it as simple as possible for easy access and entry?

Vaults can be incrementally built up. A common mistake when planning a recovery vault is *analysis paralysis*. Businesses may get bogged down in the classification of *mission-critical business functions* and not start building and populating the vault until this is known. A more sensible approach is to quickly identify the essential IT functions and essential operational data. This identification process should take days, not weeks – IT teams should be acutely aware of their essential systems, and usually only a couple of business departments (e.g., HR and payments) will need to be consulted on the operational data. Then, while the classification process for mission-critical data/functions is taking place, the vault can be built with some overhead for onboarding that data once it is identified.

What should that overhead be? While this will vary from business to business, a good rule of thumb would be to assume that the identified mission-critical data/functions will have a footprint of between 15% and 25% of the FETB of all production systems. Even if this turns out to be a conservative figure, so long as the vault is built with expandability in mind, there will still have been a good start made to the environment.

4.5.3 Running analytics on the data

Let's say you've configured an air-gapped vault and have been using a secure process to update it daily with a copy of your most critical data – the data fulfilling all three categories outlined in Section 4.5.2.

Now, let's say your security and infrastructure teams identify a destructive cyber-attack running in your production environment. Perhaps it's a form of ransomware that has been encrypting random data for days, if not weeks.

How do you know what is *safe* to recover? Being able to answer this question marks the difference between whether your vault reinforces your cyber *resilience* posture or just acts as a tertiary copy of your data.

To know whether it is safe to recover data – that you won't for instance be re-introducing compromised files (and worse, executables) into your production network – you must know which copies of data held in your vault are compromised, and which are safe. This requires scanning of the content, but vault scanning is not the same as normal product systems scanning (i.e., anti-virus tools). For one, anti-virus tools require constant updates (e.g., looking for updated virus signatures every day, sometimes more often), and the frequency of these updates is not conducive to air gaps. Additionally, anti-virus tools would already be running in your production network, so they're not providing any additional, actionable insights against vaulted data. That is, they won't catch anything new.

Anti-virus tools also tend to restrict themselves to *files*, not *behaviours*. Yes, in an ideal situation, an anti-virus tool will spot any software being used by a malicious attacker, but this won't always be the case, and there will always be a gap between the time malicious software is developed and anti-virus signatures are detected.

Cyber-attacks can be detected by scanning individual files. For instance, a file that goes from unencrypted to fully or even partially encrypted may indicate a ransomware attack. However, more subtle cyber-attacks may require pattern-based analysis of many files to properly detect. Are backups suddenly significantly increasing (or decreasing) in size? File-based attacks can be blunt-force via encryption, but they may be more subtle. This might mean leaving file headers intact and only encrypt file content, or it can leave file headers intact and destroy (e.g., by writing random data to) the remainder of the content, leaving file sizes the same.

In essence, detecting evidence of a cyber-attack moves beyond conventional anti-virus scanning into the realm of anomaly detection.

Once backup datasets have been vaulted, good vaulting practice will see the following sequence of actions take place:

1. Data is locked/made immutable for the intended retention period within the vault.
2. Data is scanned for analysis; analysis is based on:
   a. Immediate observations (e.g., "this data has been encrypted all of a sudden")
   b. Trends, and therefore anomalies (e.g., "this backup is 50% larger than expected")
3. Analysis reports are issued. These may indicate:
   a. No issues detected.
   b. No data received.
   c. Suspicious data/anomalies detected. This will include comprehensive details on the issues detected, *and* ideally the last known *good* copy of the data.

The recoverability advantage of in-vault analytics is point 3c above. If the system can identify anomalous behaviour *and* pinpoint previous copies of the same content that are safe to recover, you'll trim potentially days, if not weeks (and considerable risk) from your recovery capabilities in the event of a cyber-attack.

 LESSON TWELVE: Cyber resilience requires active scanning of vaulted data for anomaly detection. Without this, you have no reliable path forward for data recoverability. And businesses that are unable to recover may not survive a cyber-attack.

4.5.4 Recovery considerations

As discussed in the introduction, there are six broad categories of recoveries in a data protection system:

1. Operational
2. Long-term (compliance)

3. Disaster
4. Business continuity
5. Data re-use
6. Audit (test)

In an ideal situation, the only time you'll ever have to recover from a vault is to *test* recovery from the vault – i.e., to audit successful operation of the vault. Nevertheless, it's important to have considered all aspects of recovery well before needing to do so.

True recoveries from a vault are typically aligned to *business continuity* recoveries. For example, recoveries from a vault may be measured in hours or days. However, the actual restore time may be low, depending on available bandwidth and the amount of data to be restored – instead, much of the time taken may be with other processes.

Let's say vault scanning identifies potentially compromised files and issues an alert to the Security Operations Center, and the security team subsequently verifies that an attack is taking place.

If the cyber-attack is serious enough to call a halt to production operations, and data damage has been done, there will be several required steps before data can be recovered into the production environment, including but not limited to:

1. **Engaging continuity plans**: If the outage is wide-spread or has compromised key systems, it will be necessary to engage cyber continuity plans, which will be a variant of business continuity plans. In some cases, this may even mean switching certain business functions to manual (non-electronic) processing.
2. **Engaging law enforcement**: Depending on the industry vertical or local regulations, this may be required. Even if it is not legally required, it may be deemed necessary by key business stakeholders.
   a. Law enforcement teams may need time to forensically examine systems and logs. During this period, affected systems may be treated as a crime scene and be off-limits to staff and regular usage.
   b. Some equipment may even be seized by law enforcement teams as evidence.
3. **Engaging insurance teams**: If the company has cyber-insurance and plan to make a claim, insurance assessors may need to be engaged *prior* to restoring production operations. (Note that

if insurance is going to be engaged, it's likely that law enforcement will be required to help establish proof of an incident.)

4. **Network/system cleansing**: Once law enforcement and/or insurance teams are done with systems, the security and administration teams will be able to start the process of cleaning the systems of the attack. In addition to forensic auditing conducted by the security and administration teams, this is likely to also include system rebuilds for compromised servers.

5. **Systems and data restoration**: Once data and systems can be recovered safely without risk of re-infection, these activities can *start*. 'Safely' means:
   a. There should be no risk of any residual infection that may attack data once it has been recovered.
   b. Any data requiring recovery should have been had 'safe' copies identified.
   c. Data that is recovered should not re-introduce an infection to the environment.

6. **Engaging continuity failback plans** and updating digital content with any manual record-keeping that took place during the attack. (For example, if you were forced to conduct warehouse tracking by pen-and-paper for 5 days during an incident, you'll need to update your warehouse database after it has been restored.)

All of these activities take time; items 2, 3, and 4 in particular may take several days or weeks of time. Data restoration, on the other hand, may take considerably less time – at least once it can be started.

4.5.5 The value of clean rooms

Given the likelihood of a minimum multi-day delay between the time an attack is detected, and the time systems will be ready to start receiving restored data, many businesses are likely to benefit from either of the following two scenarios:

1. Pre-provisioned recovery targets *within* the vault or
2. A pre-provisioned clean room beside the vault.

Having pre-provisioned recovery targets residing within the vault will be the cheaper option and suitable for smaller or cost-constrained businesses. The number of recovery targets pre-provisioned within the vault can be variable – some businesses might only deploy a single VMware server within the vault for instance to recover just a few virtual machines onto. At minimum though there should be enough storage capacity available to restore *at least* the largest system or workload being vaulted.

By recovering onto pre-provisioned systems within the vault, you are introducing a level of risk into the vault – what if you recover a virtual machine, for instance, and that has some complex malware on it which could infect the vault if it is booted? Additionally, as we mentioned earlier in Section 4.5.1.1 and Section 4.5.1.3, vaults should operate independently of production authentication services. Recovering production systems *into* the vault may require the recovery of naming and authentication services, which could either (a) disrupt the vault or (b) result in inadvertently providing increased access to the vault.

The solution for larger or more security-conscious organisations is to use a *Clean Room* configuration that is logically isolated from the vault operations via firewalls, as shown in Figure 4.3.

Just like a clean room in a laboratory, clean rooms are self-contained areas that allow potentially dangerous activities to be conducted without compromising other locations. Within the clean room, production authentication and resolution services can be established, and operational control given to core infrastructure teams (as opposed to the vault teams), allowing workloads that had been protected by the vault to be recovered onto standby systems. These recovered workloads can be forensically examined for further review and vetting before being moved or copied back into the primary production environment. Clean rooms and other pre-provisioned systems can be used with automated processes to boost recovery velocity.

In addition to the increased security offered by clean rooms, both clean rooms and pre-provisioned systems in the vault provide a valuable recovery enhancement in the event of a cyber-attack – namely, they allow recoveries to run (at least up to the capacity of the clean room or pre-provisioned systems) *while the production environment is still under lockdown/clean-up*. Recall from Section 4.5.4 that there might be days of delays *prior* to recovery if insurance teams and/or law enforcement need to get involved – and then there's still the cleansing of the network and production systems to take place before it is safe to recover data. If data can be recovered

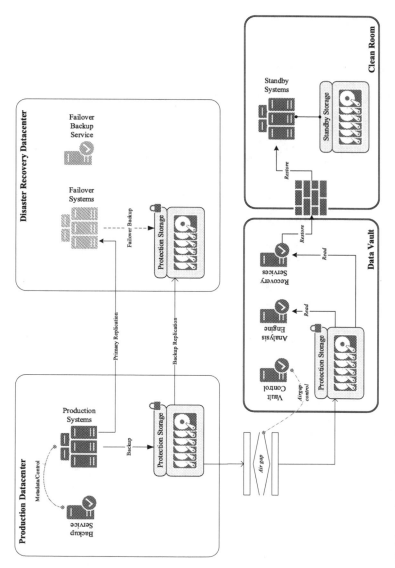

Figure 4.3 Vaulting with an adjacent clean room.

into an isolated environment while these activities are taking place, you can prepare the business for a faster transition back to regular production operations once it is safe to do so.

4.6 WRAPPING UP

Cyber-attacks are increasing in frequency and sophistication. What was once a problem faced only by select industry verticals or nation-states is now a challenge to be considered by every business operating any form of IT environment.

Switching to a pure cloud-based operation doesn't remove the risk of a cyber-attack; it just shifts the location of it. As-a-service platforms, such as SaaS (e.g., Microsoft 365), don't mitigate the risk; they just concentrate the attack surface. Operating a 'dark' site with limited or no internet connectivity can reduce the available surface area, but a single USB-key can undo all that electronic isolation, and is only suitable for certain types of businesses or operations.

In short, businesses *must* be prepared for cyber-attacks. The phrase "hope for the best but prepare for the worst" is foundational guidance for approaching a cyber-resilience strategy, and *prepare for the worst* means assuming that at some point you *will* need to recover data. Making sure that you *can* recover data in that event is therefore a critical approach to your overall security profile.

NOTES

1   NIST Cybersecurity Framework Version 1.1: https://www.nist.gov/cyberframework/framework
2   https://www.justice.gov/usao-mdla/pr/former-systems-administrator-sentenced-prison-hacking-industrial-facility-computer
3   "Hactivism: An overview plus high-profile groups and examples", Clare Stouffer, September 8 2021, https://us.norton.com/blog/emerging-threats/hacktivism
4   "Putin humiliated as hacking group infiltrates Russian state TV with Ukraine military video", Teresa Gottein Martinez, 7 March 2022, Express. https://www.express.co.uk/news/world/1576934/anonymous-hack-russia-war-ukraine-fake-news-information-ban-vladimir-putin-update

5   "The untold story of the Sony hack: How North Korea's battle with Seth Rogen and George Clooney foreshadowed Russian election meddling in 2016", Richard Stengel, October 6 2019, Vanity Fair. https://www.vanityfair.com/news/2019/10/the-untold-story-of-the-sony-hack

6   "An Unprecedented Look at Stuxnet, the World's First Digital Weapon", Kim Zetter, November 3 2014, Wired. https://www.wired.com/2014/11/countdown-to-zero-day-stuxnet/

7   "China blamed for 'massive' cyber attack on Bureau of Meteorology computer", Chris Uhlmann, December 2 2015, ABC. https://www.abc.net.au/news/2015-12-02/china-blamed-for-cyber-attack-on-bureau-of-meteorology/6993278

Chapter 5

Wrapping up

How important is it to be in a position as someone *responsible* or *accountable* for data recovery that you *know* business requirements can be met?

After talking about *the business* for the entire book, I'm going to pivot. Who cares? The business is a business. But *you* are a living, breathing person with needs and desires – and I assume one of those desires is to achieve a certain level of happiness in your life.

"Chronic stress disrupts nearly every system in your body. It can suppress your immune system, upset your digestive and reproductive systems, increase the risk of heart attack and stroke, and speed up the aging process. It can even rewire the brain, leaving you more vulnerable to anxiety, depression, and other mental health problems."

"Stress Symptoms, Signs and Causes", HelpGuide. https://www.help guide.org/articles/stress/stress-symptoms-signs-and-causes.htm

---

When you're accountable or responsible for data recovery and know there are gaps or risks, you'll be carrying a level of stress that is detrimental to your physical, emotional, and mental health.

I've been there. I spent 12 months as an engineering manager at a company that was circling the drain trying to keep broken hardware operational to keep backups running. There was no budget, so I'd spend a day in the office doing my day job, then another half day at home every night, dialled in, nursing faulty tape libraries and tape drives with insufficient capacity.

Data recoverability has largely moved on from tape libraries and drives. In some areas, this has introduced efficient simplicity into environments – an elimination of many moving parts and an ability to consume services on demand. However, we continue to see at times explosive outward growth in the complexities we face with data recoverability: workload proliferation, varied consumption models, and shrinking protection times are challenging enough, without the constant threat of malicious cyber-attacks that are now part of the modern IT reality.

If data protection isn't done right, with an allocated budget commensurate to the importance of the data to the business, it's stressful and wasteful, and is detrimental, not only to the recoverability posture of the company, but to your health and mental well-being.

As an employee of a company, you may owe it to the company to get recoverability right, but as a person who deserves a happy life with a minimum of stress, you owe it to yourself, too.

It is perhaps pertinent to close by returning our focus to the lessons noted throughout the book:

- Lesson 1: It's *when*, not *if* bad things will happen and a recovery is required.
- Lesson 2: The journey to a resilient data recovery model within your organisation starts by recognising the gaps you have in your model.
- Lesson 3: Simple, cheap, flexible: when it comes to data recoverability, you can only ever choose two.
- Lesson 4: A machine can neither be responsible nor accountable for data protection in your environment.
- Lesson 5: Data resiliency can only come from the synergistic application of fault tolerance, availability, redundancy, and recoverability. It cannot come from a subset of the pillars, no matter how strongly you build them up.
- Lesson 6: Nothing corrupts faster than a mirror.
- Lesson 7: Fault tolerance, availability, redundancy, and recoverability all depend on robustness to deliver a reliable data protection architecture.
- Lesson 8: You protect business functions and workloads. *Data* protection is a side-effect.
- Lesson 9: Public cloud doesn't eliminate the need for data resilient architecture; it just moves the work to a different location.

- Lesson 10: No technology can save your business from an untrained user with privileged access who doesn't know how to use the environment you've placed them in.
- Lesson 11: A cyber resiliency plan that doesn't include recovery is not a plan at all.
- Lesson 12: Cyber resilience requires active scanning of vaulted data for anomaly detection. Without this, you have no reliable path forward for data recoverability. And businesses that are unable to recover may not survive a cyber-attack.

Index

Pages in *italics* refer to figures, pages in **bold** refer to tables, and pages followed by 'n' refer to notes.

Printed in the United States
by Baker & Taylor Publisher Services